JAMES

HANDS-ON CHRISTIANITY

From the Bible-Teaching Ministry of

CHARLES R. SWINDOLL

INSIGHT *for* LIVING

Insight for Living's Bible teacher, Chuck Swindoll, has devoted his life to the clear, practical application of God's Word and His grace. A pastor at heart, Chuck has served as senior pastor to congregations in Texas, Massachusetts, and California. He currently leads Stonebriar Community Church in Frisco, Texas, but Chuck's listening audience extends far beyond a local church body. As a leading program in Christian broadcasting, *Insight for Living* airs around the world in major Christian radio markets and to a growing webcast audience, reaching churched and unchurched people groups in a language they can understand. Chuck's extensive writing ministry has also served the body of Christ worldwide, and his leadership as president and now chancellor of Dallas Theological Seminary has helped prepare and equip a new generation for ministry. Chuck and Cynthia, his partner in life and ministry, have four grown children and ten grandchildren.

Based on the original outlines, charts, and transcripts of Charles R. Swindoll's sermons, these messages were originally presented as part of a larger series titled *James: Practical and Authentic Living*, which combined messages on the book of James with appropriate practical Old Testament applications. In 2001, the Old Testament applications were separated from the James series and put into a smaller series titled *Practical Christianity*.

In 2003, the original messages on the book of James were put into a series and titled *James: Hands-on Christianity*. Lee Hough, a graduate of The University of Texas at Arlington and Dallas Theological Seminary, in 1991 wrote the study guide text titled *James: Practical and Authentic Living*. In 2003 those chapters were revised by the creative ministries department of Insight for Living.

Editor in Chief:
  Cynthia Swindoll
Study Guide Writers:
  Lee Hough
  Suzanne Keffer
Rights and Permissions:
  The Meredith Agency

Editors:
  Amy LaFuria
  Maridee Dietzel
  Greg Smith
Typographer:
  Bob Haskins

Unless otherwise identified, all Scripture references are from the *New American Standard Bible* © The Lockman Foundation 1960, 1962, 1963, 1968, 1971, 1972, 1973, 1975, 1977, 1995. Used by permission. Scripture taken from the *Holy Bible*, New International Version, Copyright © 1973, 1978, 1984 International Bible Society, used by permission of Zondervan Bible Publishers [NIV]. The other translations cited are the *Amplified Bible* [AMPLIFIED], the King James Version [KJV], *The Living Bible* [LB], J. B. Phillips: *The New Testament in Modern English* [PHILLIPS], and the *New English Bible* [NEB].

ISBN 1-57972-541-4
Cover design: Alex Pasieka
Cover image: © Mark Tomalty/Masterfile

CONTENTS

INTRODUCTION

Ever read about some person you wish you could sit down and talk to? Or, more often, haven't you come across the writings of a particular individual you'd love to spend an evening with? One of those people in my life is James. I am really drawn to this guy! He is practical. He is insightful. He is also gutsy, honest, and sincere to the core. He's a rare find today.

This study we are about to undertake will reveal just how true all these things are. You will find yourself thinking, *The man has been looking through my keyhole!* It is remarkable how penetrating and convicting the letter is . . . even though it was written around the middle of the first century.

Make me a promise, okay? Stay open and teachable. Don't resist the message of James, especially when he probes into the nerve center of your walk and your talk. He's right on target, pinpointing the very things that need our attention.

Someday we will be able to sit down and talk with James. When we do, it will be great to tell him how much we appreciated what he wrote, won't it?

Chuck Swindoll

Charles R. Swindoll

PUTTING TRUTH
INTO ACTION

Knowledge apart from application falls short of God's desire for His children. He wants us to apply what we learn so that we will change and grow. This study guide was prepared with these goals in mind. As you go through the following pages, we hope your desire to discover biblical truth will grow as your understanding of God's Word increases and that you will be encouraged to apply what you've learned.

To assist you in your study, we've included a section called *Living Insights* at the end of each lesson. These exercises will challenge you to study further and to think of specific ways to put your discoveries into action.

We've also added **Questions for Group Discussion,** which are formulated to get your group talking and sharing ideas about the key issues in each lesson.

There are many ways to use this guide—in personal devotions, group studies, discussions with friends and family, and Sunday school classes. And, of course, it's an ideal study aid when you're listening to its corresponding *Insight for Living* radio series.

To benefit most from this study guide, we would encourage you to consider it a spiritual journal. That's why we've included space in the Living Insights section for recording your thoughts and discoveries. We hope you'll return to those sections often for review and encouragement as you continue to grow in your walk with Christ.

Insight for Living

JAMES

HANDS-ON CHRISTIANITY

Chapter 1

A CASE FOR PRACTICAL CHRISTIANITY

Survey of James

The Bible dwells on two prominent themes in its sixty-six books: the way to God and the walk with God. While many books of the Bible are directed to the lost (those dead in sin), telling them how they can find God, it may surprise you to know that the majority of Scripture is directed toward the saint, or the one who walks with God. The book of James leads its New Testament counterparts in this second category, challenging those who already know God to boldly walk with Him.

For those of us who have already found the *way to God* (through faith in Jesus Christ), James delivers practical guidelines for Christian living. The book of James tells us where the "rubber meets the road." It gets down to where we live. Often compared with the Old Testament book of Proverbs, this crash course in Christianity offers pithy exhortations, maxims, and wise sayings about how to live for God. James is a unique book, a compact travel guide for the Christian journey that fits better in a biker's pack than on a theologian's bookshelf.

Generally speaking, the book of James is not meant to be a great doctrinal treatise. The name of the Lord Jesus Christ appears only twice, and the author never mentions the Cross, the Resurrection, or the Holy Spirit. But this letter wasn't written to establish the doctrines of the faith. It was written to drive home the importance of living out the truth. In essence, the main issue that prompted James to write was this: If you say you believe, why do you act like you don't? James is a book that will challenge you to examine your

1

life. It's not a book that brings a few simple rebukes, but a book that assaults us in any area in which we profess to have faith but fail to show any evidence of that faith in our lives.

Before we begin our study of this book, let's acquaint ourselves with some important background information.

The Writer

The writer identifies himself as simply "James, a bond-servant of God and of the Lord Jesus Christ" (James 1:1). But which James? The New Testament mentions five men living in the first century who bore the same name. Most conservative New Testament scholars agree that this James was Jesus' half brother, born and raised in the same family.[1]

His History

For centuries the erroneous notion has persisted that Mary and Joseph had no other children besides Jesus. But, according to Matthew 13:54–56, Jesus had several siblings.

> He came to His hometown and began teaching them in their synagogue, so that they were astonished, and said, "Where did this man get this wisdom and these miraculous powers? Is not this the carpenter's son? Is not His mother called Mary, and His brothers, James and Joseph and Simon and Judas? And His sisters, are they not all with us?"

James grew up with the formidable challenge of following in the footsteps of his sinless older brother Jesus. Growing up in the shadow of perfection couldn't have been a picnic in the park. And things didn't get any easier for James in adulthood, when his controversial older brother came home claiming to be the Messiah.

---

1. "There is the James who was the father of the member of the Twelve called Judas, not Iscariot (Luke 6:16). . . . There is James, the son of Alphaeus, who was a member of the Twelve (Matthew 10:3; Mark 3:18; Luke 6:15; Acts 1:13). . . . There is the James who is called James the Younger and is mentioned in Mark 15:40. . . . There is James, the brother of John, and the son of Zebedee, a member of the Twelve (Matthew 10:2; Mark 3:17; Luke 6:14; Acts 1:13). . . . Finally, there is James, who is called the brother of Jesus. Although the first definite connection of him with this letter does not emerge until Origen in the first half of the third century, it is to him that it [the letter] has always been traditionally ascribed." William Barclay, *The Letters of James and Peter*, rev. ed., The Daily Study Bible series (Philadelphia, Pa.: Westminster Press, 1976), pp. 8–9.

How did James and other family members react? Mark 3:21 tells us.

> When His own people heard of this, they went out
> to take custody of Him; for they were saying, "He
> has lost His senses."

The Living Bible says, "He's out of His mind." J. B. Phillips translates, "He must be mad." The decided opinion of the family, apparently including James, was, "He's a nut!" John 7:5 states, "For not even His brothers were believing in Him."

As far as we know, James's unbelief persisted even to the time of Jesus' death on the cross. But 1 Corinthians 15:1–7 tells us that, afterward, the resurrected Lord Jesus visited James, and from that moment on, James appears in the Scriptures as a different man. In fact, he became one of the early church's most significant leaders, serving the Lord until he was stoned to death in A.D. 62.[2]

His Perspective

It is interesting to note that in the introduction to his letter, James does not identify himself by saying, "I am Jesus' brother." He could have done that, but it would have been name-dropping, something James condemns later in his letter as a phony and empty practice. Instead, James identifies himself as "a bond-servant of God and of the Lord Jesus Christ" (James 1:1). He recognized that his real relationship to Jesus was not physical but spiritual, made possible by the grace of God alone.

His Relationship to His Readers

In James 1:2 and throughout the letter, James identifies his readers as "brethren." He uses this word in a way that means more than just "my fellow Jews." It specifically referred to Jewish followers of Christ.

James also referred to these people as being "dispersed abroad" (v. 1), meaning "scattered throughout," as one might scatter seed. There's a reason for this. James was writing in about A.D. 45, when Claudius was emperor of Rome. Under his rule the Jews had been persecuted and driven out of Rome and their homeland, Palestine. Jewish businesses were boycotted, Jewish children were mocked and thrown out of schools. Life was grim, threatening, and unsafe.

---

2. According to Flavius Josephus, as quoted by J. Ronald Blue in "James" in *The Bible Knowledge Commentary*, New Testament ed., ed. John F. Walvoord and Roy B. Zuck (Wheaton, Ill.: SP Publications, Victor Books, 1983), p. 816.

Someone has said that "persecution purifies," but constant suffering crushes. That's exactly what happened to many early Christian Jews. They buckled under the pressure of constant persecution. With their words they professed to believe, but with their actions they denied the Savior.

In this milieu of suffering and defection, James penned a powerful letter of exhortation and encouragement. His letter was not about doctrines and precepts, but about maintaining a faithful practice of the Christian faith. His words brought answers to the community of faith, the saints who felt crushed under the load of persecution.

The Book as a Whole

Now let's turn our attention from the author to the book itself. We'll glimpse its unique features and get a brief overview of its contents.

The Main Theme

The heart of James's message can be summed up in these words: Genuine faith produces genuine works. If you say you've come to know the Lord Jesus, then your life should reflect that commitment.

The Main Section

The pivotal section of this book is 2:14–20. The book's major thrust is contained in verse 14.

> What use is it, my brethren, if someone says he has faith but he has no works? Can that faith save him?

Anyone can claim to be a Christian, but James points out that a person who has genuinely found faith will display it in his or her daily life. He illustrates this principle with a down-to-earth example.

> If a brother or sister is without clothing and in need of daily food, and one of you says to them, "Go in peace, be warmed and be filled," and yet you do not give them what is necessary for their body, what use is that? (vv. 15–16)

James is not advocating salvation by works, as some have accused him. Rather, he's advocating a salvation *accompanied by* works. Faith is the root; works are the fruit. Without fruit, which is the evidence of faith working in our lives, our words about faith are empty and lifeless. "Even so faith, if it has no works, is dead, being by itself. . . . But are you willing to recognize, you foolish fellow, that faith without works is useless?" (vv. 17, 20)

An Overview

The following outline of the book's four sections, together with the chart at the beginning of this lesson, gives us an idea of the progression of James.

James 1. In chapter 1 James asserts that when real faith is stretched, it doesn't break. Rather, it produces stability. To prove his point, James uses three examples. In verses 2–12 he shows us that life's trials don't squash faith, they cause real faith to emerge. In verses 13–16 he reminds us we can hold fast to our faith through every temptation. And in verses 17–27 he explains that when the true believer is confronted with the truth of Scripture, he or she will respond by conforming to what it teaches.

James 2. The theme throughout this section is that when real faith is pressed, it doesn't fail. Instead, it produces genuine love. When we are crushed in the winepress of life, love is the sweet juice that flows forth from us. Real faith fights against prejudice (vv. 1–13), indifference (vv. 14–20), and dry intellectual belief (vv. 21–26). Real faith has grit to it. It fights for what is right, and it can stand up under any test.

James 3–4. Here James affirms that genuine faith is expressed with control and humility, not arrogance. He goes on to address the ways we express our faith: verbally (3:1–12), emotionally (3:13–4:12), and volitionally (4:13–17).

James 5. The final emphasis of this letter on Christian living is that when real faith is distressed, it doesn't panic. Instead, it produces patience. James illustrates this message through everyday situations: how we should deal with money matters (vv. 1–12), with sickness (vv. 13–18), and with a fellow Christian who isn't walking with the Lord (vv. 19–20).

Our Relationship to His Message

The first-century Christians were struggling, and they needed some straight talk from someone who could help them reform. Today many of us need that same clear-cut guidance. Our vocabularies are bulging with all the right words, but our lifestyles are anemic from lack of spiritual substance. We may "know the way,"

5

but we need to be stirred to "walk in the way." James is a book that will do just that. It will

> prick the conscience of every dull, defeated, and degenerated Christian in the world. Here is a "right stirring epistle" designed to exhort and encourage, to challenge and convict, to rebuke and revive, to describe practical holiness and drive believers toward the goal of a faith that works. James is severely ethical and refreshingly practical.[3]

Living Insights

A quick survey of the book of James reveals a Christian primer filled with practical advice about living the Christian life, facing trials and temptations, being "quick to hear, slow to speak and slow to anger" (James 1:19). It teaches us about self-control and humility, planting seeds of patience and common sense along the path.

A practical faith produces results that are genuine and lasting. Before we dig into the specifics of this book, let's take some time to reflect on our own journey with Christ. Take a moment to recall the moments of profound change in your walk with the Lord: the moment of salvation, significant decisions along the way, and times when trusting in Christ led you closer to Him. Chart your journey with Christ on the timeline that follows, beginning with your earliest faith memories and ending with your current relationship with Him.

1. If you have already received Christ as Lord and Savior, place a cross over the time in your life when this occurred. If you are still in the process of evaluating your relationship with Christ, place an asterisk above the line as a reminder to return to this point of decision as you progress through this study.

2. Indicate the moment(s) in your life when you felt closest to God by writing a brief reminder of this experience in the space above the line.

3. Indicate the moment(s) in your life when you felt distant from God by writing a brief reminder of this experience in the space below the line.

3. Blue, "James," p. 815.

6

CHILDHOOD	ADOLESCENCE	TEEN YEARS	YOUNG ADULT	MIDDLE YEARS	MATURITY

Conclude this time of reflection by reading through James's letter as though it were written specifically to you.

 Questions for Group Discussion

The most controversial topic in the book of James is its teaching on faith and works.[4] Urging Christians to act on what they believe, James challenges us to a deeper walk with the Lord. Right belief coupled with right behavior produces genuine results.

1. James challenges us to act on what we believe as a demonstration of our true faith. Do your actions match your faith? If so, how? If not, discuss the area(s) of your life you would like to change.

2. How do you think someone like James, with his insistence on practical Christianity, would be received in your church today? In most churches?

3. Regarding the relationship between faith and works, discuss any initial assumptions you bring to this study. How does your perspective differ from that of other members of the group?

4. How is this letter relevant to your daily life?

5. What do you hope to gain as you study the book of James?

---

4. Buist M. Fanning, "A Theology of James," in *A Biblical Theology of the New Testament*, ed. Roy B. Zuck, consulting ed. Darrell L. Bock (Chicago, Ill.: Moody Press, 1994), p. 423.

Chapter 2

WHEN TROUBLES WON'T GO AWAY
James 1:2–12

As children, we'd watch our favorite action heroes on TV resolving unthinkable dilemmas in a half-hour program. Before the preview of coming episodes faded to black, we'd crash through the screen door, bringing this week's adventure to life, casting ourselves in the role of Superman, the Incredible Hulk, Wonder Woman, or one of countless other imaginary characters. Scraped knees and bruised elbows were simply hazards of living the imaginary life of a superhero. Mistakes could be reconciled with a creative plot twist, often rooted in youthful imagination. Trouble had a way of disappearing along with the setting sun.

As adults, we still make mistakes and "scrape our knees," but manipulating life's storyline to our advantage becomes more difficult. We get the wind knocked out of us by unfaithful marriage partners, crippling accidents, or the sudden death of someone close. We may have traded climbing trees for climbing corporate ladders, but it still hurts when we fall. We don't cut our fingers much anymore, but we do hurt from cutting remarks that leave us bleeding on the inside. Nowadays it's our hearts, not our elbows and knees, that reveal the signs of trouble. The day's cuts, burns, and spills leave behind painful emotional welts. We often feel as if we were, in Shakespeare's words, "a wretched soul, bruised with adversity."[1]

Adversity—it besets us all. A battered and melancholy Job sighed, "Man . . . is short-lived and full of turmoil" (Job 14:1). Even David, who enjoyed an enviable closeness with God, confessed, "Many are the afflictions of the righteous" (Ps. 34:19). And Paul explained, "We are afflicted in every way, . . . perplexed, . . . persecuted, . . . struck down . . ." (2 Cor. 4:8–9). Someone has said that if you were to trace Paul's journeys in the first century, it would be like tracking the path of a wounded deer running from a hunter, leaving one bloody trail after another.

---

1. William Shakespeare, *The Comedy of Errors*, act 2, scene 1, line 34.

In our last chapter, we saw James addressing Jewish Christians who were literally bruised with adversity. They were being hunted under the persecution instigated by the Roman emperor, Claudius. They had been driven from their homes and homeland and were constantly being treated with hostility—by Gentiles, who hated them because they were Jewish, and by fellow Jews, who hated them for being Christians. These believers knew the bruised and blood-stained misery of troubles that wouldn't go away. Against this back-drop colored by first century trials, James describes the truth about troubles for those who are bruised with adversity.

What Is True About Troubles?

Today there are numerous ideas being tossed around regarding trials. Some people believe they're a form of punishment from God. Others dangle the promise before us that if we can just reach a certain level of maturity, trials will disappear and we'll live the "abundant" life. And still others are out there trying to convince us that there's really no such thing as adversity. There are erroneous claims that trials, such as sickness or pain, are forms of negative confessions rooted in our lack of faith; they don't exist in the life of true believers.

James, however, has something quite different to say about trials.

Trials Are Inevitable

> Consider it all joy, my brethren, when you encounter various trials . . . (James 1:2)

Notice that James didn't say, "Consider it all joy *if* you encounter various trials." He said *when*. We needn't wonder if they'll come or when they'll leave. They're here to stay (compare 1 Peter 4:12). James also gives us fair warning about the kinds of trials we can expect. The Greek word he uses for "various" is the one from which we get the term *polka dot*. By this he means that we can expect our lives to be spattered with trials of all sizes and shapes.

Trials Have Purpose

> . . . knowing that the testing of your faith produces endurance. And let endurance have its perfect result, so that you may be perfect and complete, lacking in nothing. (James 1:3–4)

Trials do have a purpose. But before we can grasp what that purpose is, we've got to give up viewing troubles as simply bothersome offenses and start seeing them as tests—tests specifically designed by God to stretch our faith, not simply our pocketbooks, friendships, or health. Rather than viewing them as our enemies, we should look upon these tests as servants that bring about the circumstances needed to help us grow.

God isn't interested in watching our faith get torpedoed by trials. What He does desire becomes clear when we understand the meaning of the word *testing* (v. 3). It comes from the Greek term *dokimos*, which means "approval." It's a word found on the undersides of many ancient pieces of pottery unearthed by archeologists in the Near East. This mark meant that the piece had gone through the furnace without cracking; it had been approved. God's desire is to help the clay vessels created in His image to mature in the furnace of trials without a crack.

In every trial, God's initial purpose is to produce *endurance*. This word comes from a combination of two words that, put together, literally mean "to abide under." God's seal of approval, *dokimos*, is applied to those who persevere, or abide under, the tests He sends. God directs specific tests to stretch us spiritually. He arranges particular troubles to challenge us, not hoping we will go under but with the desire that we learn to exhibit a great character quality: *endurance*. Enduring those tests is what brings about the maturity that is God's ultimate purpose for our lives (v. 4).

How Can I Rise Above Troubles?

Speaking from his experience as a prisoner in the Nazi concentration camps, psychiatrist Dr. Viktor Frankl said,

> Everything can be taken from a man but one thing:
> the last of the human freedoms—to choose one's
> attitude in any given set of circumstances, to choose
> one's own way.[2]

Trials can strip away everything but our attitude toward them. Let's briefly go back over the verses we've just covered and consider three key elements, elements that form the attitude God wants us to choose when we face a trial.

2. Viktor E. Frankl, *Man's Search for Meaning*, revised and updated (Canton, N.Y.: Beacon Press, 1959; New York, N.Y.: Pocket Books, Washington Square Press, 1984), p. 86.

Consider It All Joy

The word *consider* (v. 2) in its original form literally means "to lead the way"; it's the idea of going ahead of something else. Here it is linked together with the attitude of joy. The Christian's mindset, going into a trial, is to be positive.[3] When surrounded by the trials of life, we should respond with joy. "Most people count it all joy when they *escape* trials. James said to count it all joy in the midst of trials."[4]

Knowing That the Testing . . . Produces Endurance

How can a believer be joyful, positive, and assured in the midst of a trial? Because we *know* (v. 3), or "comprehend," that tests are designed by God for good, not evil. We know that they have a purpose and that we aren't simply "playthings of circumstance."[5] The heat of the furnace is not designed to make us crack, but to solidify and strengthen His character in us.

Let Endurance Have Its Perfect Result

The third key term, found in verse 4, is *let*, meaning "cooperate." Give in to the testing. Allow it to do its job in your life. Participate in the lessons the trial brings to teach you. James illustrates his challenge in verses 9–11:

> But the brother of humble circumstances is to glory in his high position; and the rich man is to glory in his humiliation, because like flowering grass he will pass away. For the sun rises with a scorching wind and withers the grass; and its flower falls off and the beauty of its appearance is destroyed; so too the rich man in the midst of his pursuits will fade away.

---

3. Let's be careful about what James is saying here. He's not advocating that Christians should deny the pain and sorrow they feel in the midst of a trial. "Indeed, [J.B.] Mayor points out that James does not say that trial is all joy; rather, he urges his readers to *count* it all joy, 'that is, look at it from the bright side, as capable of being turned to our highest good.'" Curtis Vaughn, *James: A Study Guide* (Grand Rapids, Mich.: Zondervan Publishing House, 1969), p. 18.

4. J. Ronald Blue, "James," in *The Bible Knowledge Commentary*, New Testament ed., ed. John F. Walvoord and Roy B. Zuck (Wheaton, Ill.: SP Publications, Victor Books, 1983), p. 820.

5. Frankl, *Man's Search for Meaning*, p. 87.

Both the brother who has nothing and the rich man with everything are challenged to do the same thing: *Let the test go on, regardless of your circumstances*. Don't cut short the process that will bring about your maturity.

Why Do Troubles Overwhelm Us?

All of us know what it's like to flunk a trial. We remember the wrong responses—resistant attitudes or temper tantrums demanding instant relief—that have advanced nothing but our immaturity and misery. Why do we do these things? Why don't we hang in there? James offers two reasons why our troubles often get the best of us.

Lack of Wisdom

When troubles arrive with a surprising knock at life's door, we may not be prepared to handle them. Like an unwelcome guest, our trials can cause our best-laid plans to fall into disarray. But the face of adversity need not cause us to surrender. James says to pray for help:

> But if any of you lacks wisdom, let him ask of God,
> who gives to all generously and without reproach,
> and it will be given to him. (v. 5)

The wisdom mentioned here is directly related to trials; it's not just wisdom in general. James is referring to the ability to view a test from God's perspective. Without this kind of wisdom, the ability to endure becomes elusive, and the goal of maturity may never be reached.

Lack of Faith

The second reason why trials overwhelm us is a lack of faith.

> But he must ask in faith without any doubting, for
> the one who doubts is like the surf of the sea, driven
> and tossed by the wind. For that man ought not to
> expect that he will receive anything from the Lord,
> being a double-minded man, unstable in all his ways.
> (vv. 6–8)

James is not referring to saving faith, nor to a general kind of trust. He's advocating a sustaining faith that involves complete abandonment to God and His purposes in our trials.

Verse 8 gives us a name for someone to whom wisdom just doesn't get through—that person's called "double-minded." A double-minded person is someone who wants his or her own will and God's at the same time. Someone who, down inside, still has reservations about being completely yielded to God.

What Is Promised to Those Who Handle Problems Correctly?

> Blessed is a man who perseveres under trial; for once he has been approved, he will receive the crown of life which the Lord has promised to those who love Him. (v. 12)

Those who endure the trials of life are promised at least two rewards. The first promise is of happiness, as we learn from the term *blessed*, which means "genuinely happy." In the Old Testament, the word *blessing* is always used in the plural, signifying being happy many times over. This kind of happiness is impossible if it's dependent on circumstances, but it's available in abundance if we depend on the Lord in all our circumstances.

The second promise is of "the crown of life"—a future reward in heaven for those who endure trials because of their love of Christ. But James isn't referring just to a future crown to be received once we're in heaven; he's referring to the crown of a rich and full life to be enjoyed here and now. Historian and theologian William Barclay draws out several of the implications hidden in James's reference to this crown of life.

> In the ancient world, the crown (*stephanos*) had at least four great associations.
> (a) The crown of flowers was worn at times of joy . . . [it] was the sign of happy and festive joy.
> (b) The crown was the mark of royalty. It was worn by kings and by those in authority. . . .
> (c) The crown of laurel leaves was the victor's crown in the games, the prize which the athlete coveted above all. . . .
> (d) The crown was the mark of honor and of dignity. . . .
> The Christian has a *joy* that no other man can ever have. . . . The Christian has a *royalty* that other men have never realized, for however humble

his earthly circumstances, he is nothing less than a child of God. The Christian has a *victory* which others cannot win, for he meets life and all its demands in the conquering power of the presence and company of Jesus Christ. . . . The Christian has a new *dignity*, for he is ever conscious that God thought him worth the life and death of Jesus Christ. No man can ever be worthless, if Christ died for him.[6]

A Concluding Thought

James wrote the opening passages of his letter for those whom Shakespeare would call "wretched souls, bruised by adversity." In fact, they are written for all of us. Some bruises are deeper and last longer than others, but we're all bruised. We find our solution in God's Son, Jesus Christ, who endured the bruising, the hate, and the sin of man. In Him we do not find relief from our trials, but the strength to endure them, that we might be known as one approved by God. Nietzsche said, "He who has a *why* to live can bear with almost any *how*."[7] James has given us the why about our adversities . . . and now we can do more than just *bear* our trials; we can actually choose to *grow* through them!

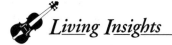 *Living Insights*

In *Hope Again: When Life Hurts and Dreams Fade*, Chuck Swindoll writes,

> If you're experiencing trials, you're the rule, not the exception. If you have just gotten through one, take heart, there are more around the corner! Going through a trial is one thing that pulls us together. We've got that in common.
>
> They may be physical, emotional, financial, or spiritual. They may slip in unexpectedly and knock on the door of your business, your church, or your

---

6. William Barclay, *The Letters of James and Peter*, rev. ed., The Daily Study Bible series (Philadelphia, Pa.: Westminster Press, 1976), pp. 48–49.

7. Friedrich Wilhelm Nietzsche, as quoted by Frankl in *Man's Search for Meaning*, p. 12.

home. They may arrive at any time or at any season. They may come suddenly, like a car accident or a natural catastrophe. They may be prolonged, like a drawn-out court case or a lingering, nagging illness. Trials can be public in nature or very private. They can be directly related to our own sin, the sin of others, or not related to sin at all.

A trial can be like a rock hitting the water. You don't cause the jolt, but you're impacted by it. You're just standing there, and suddenly the smooth lake of your life surges into giant waves and almost drowns you.[8]

Do you feel like you're drowning in trials? What are some of the giant waves that may be threatening to take you under?

_____

_____

_____

In response to our trials, James comforts us with the hope that our struggles are not in vain; they have purpose (James 1:2–12). What character traits are developed as we encounter trials in our lives? (vv. 3–5)

_____

_____

_____

Failure to persevere may bring compromise as we question God's goodness and chafe against His sovereignty. What are some of the consequences of doubting God's character during trials? (vv. 6–8)

_____

_____

_____

8. Charles R. Swindoll, *Hope Again: When Life Hurts and Dreams Fade* (Dallas, Tex.: Word Publishing, 1996), p. 201.

Spiritual maturity, forged on the anvil of trials, earns heavenly rewards that are life's truest treasure. According to commentator William Barclay, the rewards that God promises through trials are some of the few things we can count on to last:

> If life is so uncertain and man so vulnerable, calamity and disaster may come at any moment. Since that is so, a man is foolish to put all his trust in things— like wealth—which he may lose at any moment. He is only wise if he puts his trust in things which he cannot lose.[9]

One way to capture the essence of a passage is to paraphrase a few of the main ideas. Personalize James 1:12 by writing it in your own words, emphasizing the results of testing for you.

_____

_____

_____

_____

 Questions for Group Discussion

James 1:2–12 is a very comforting passage . . . especially to those experiencing some sort of difficulty. In a small group there are inevitably a few people struggling with problems in their personal life. Some struggle with difficult relationships at work, at home, even at church. Others face personal health concerns or illnesses within their families. Some have significant questions about their faith in God. We all struggle with trials in one form or another. James tells us there is a purpose behind our trials. And yet, most of us would prefer to forgo the test altogether.

1. To ease into a discussion about our personal trials, have a member of the group volunteer to share a past experience where they were tested . . . with positive results. What character qualities were being tested in this situation? How did God reveal Himself in this situation? What were some life changes that resulted from enduring this trial?

9. William Barclay, *The Letters of James and Peter*, p. 48.

2. There are times when we struggle to know God's direction or purpose in a given situation. How should we approach God, seeking His wisdom and guidance, in these situations? (v. 5)

3. Asking God to intervene in our lives is an act of faith. James says we must believe and not doubt (v. 6). When you pray, do you pray in faith with confidence, or is there an element of doubt? Discuss your thoughts with the group.

4. In *The Hiding Place*, Corrie ten Boom writes, "There is no pit so deep but He is not deeper still."[10] In this section of James, we see trials of various kinds and tests of faith designed to develop our maturity, that we may be "complete, lacking in nothing" (v. 4). God meets us at the point of our deepest need. Where is God meeting you today? What challenges are you facing in this season of life? Discuss how your faith is currently being shaped by the trials and tests of daily life.

10. Corrie ten Boom, *The Hiding Place* (New York, N.Y.: Bantam Books, 1971), p. 217.

Chapter 3

PLAIN TALK ABOUT TEMPTATION

James 1:13–18

Mark Antony was known as the silver-tongued orator of Rome. He was a brilliant man, a strong leader, and a courageous soldier, but the one thing he lacked was strength of character. On the outside he was powerful and impressive, but on the inside he was weak and vulnerable. This so enraged his tutor that on occasion he shouted at him, "O Marcus! O colossal child, able to conquer the world but unable to resist a temptation."[1]

That indictment fits not only Mark Antony but also many of us today. No one is immune to the bewitching appeals of temptation's sirens. And some, like Mark Antony, find it virtually impossible to resist the pull of their alluring voices.

Countless people have wrecked their lives on the jagged reefs of sin, drawn in by temptation's seductive song. Temptation involves all types of sin and all types of people. Parents, grandparents, students and professionals alike are constantly being wooed to destruction by sin's enticements. Many friendships lay battered and broken apart on the rocks where gossip sings. And floating face down beneath the choral urgings of power and popularity are the washed-out lives of leaders, pastors, teens, parents, executives, politicians—people who veered off course from following God and toward the tempting promise of fulfillment some other way. Perhaps you have fallen and struggle with escaping sin's grasp. How will you learn to stay on course?

According to Greek mythology, the crew on Odysseus's ship escaped the lure of the Sirens' beguiling voices by stopping their ears with wax. Our lives faces an equal peril.

> In our members there is a slumbering inclination towards desire which is both sudden and fierce. With irresistible power desire seizes mastery over the flesh. All at once a secret, smoldering fire is kindled. The

---

1. Charles R. Swindoll, *The Tale of the Tardy Oxcart and 1,501 Other Stories* (Nashville, Tenn.: Word Publishing, Inc., 1998), p. 562.

flesh burns and is in flames. It makes no difference whether it is sexual desire, or ambition, or vanity, or desire for revenge, or love of fame and power, or greed for money. . . . Joy in God is in course of being extinguished in us and we seek all our joy in the creature.[2]

Unfortunately, resisting the kind of real-life temptation that Dietrich Bonhoeffer describes will take more than earplugs. The book of James fills our ears, not with wax, but with important insights and truths about temptation—knowledge that will enable us to sail past temptation's call.

Facts about Temptation

As we begin, let's establish what we mean by temptation. The dictionary defines *tempt* this way: "to entice to do wrong by promise of pleasure or gain."[3] It holds the idea of seduction, or alluring into evil, and, more subtly, persuasion. It is an allurement with sinister motives. Adding to this basic understanding, James presents us with four facts that we must all understand before we can even begin to deal with the problem.

Temptation Is Always Present in Life

Let no one say when he is tempted . . .
(James 1:13a)

Notice the verse doesn't say "if" we are tempted, but "when." The moment we entered this world, we were drafted into a lifelong battle with temptation. A monk living behind the monastery wall is as much assaulted by it as the person who works in a busy downtown office. Being tempted is not a sin—even Jesus Himself was tempted—but giving in to temptation is. We are held accountable for our actions and reactions to temptation.

Temptation Is Never Prompted by God

Let no one say when he is tempted, "I am being tempted by God"; for God cannot be tempted by evil, and He Himself does not tempt anyone. (v. 13)

2. Dietrich Bonhoeffer, *Creation and Fall and Temptation* (New York, N.Y.: Collier Books, Macmillan Publishing Co., 1959), p. 116.

3. Merriam-Webster's Collegiate Dictionary, 10th ed., see "tempt."

In his commentary on James, Curtis Vaughan points out that

> man is naturally inclined to shift the blame from himself to God for his moral failures. One needs only to recall the words of Adam after he was charged with the first sin committed on earth: "And the man said, The woman *whom thou gavest to be with me*, she gave me of the tree, and I did eat" (Genesis 3:12). In every age since, men have tried to cast the burden of guilt off of themselves and put the blame on God.[4]

In the Greek language, there are two different words used for the English word *by*. James's choice in verse 13 strengthens his message that we are not tempted by God. He could have used the Greek preposition *hupo*, which would have indicated that God is not directly responsible for temptation. Instead, James uses *apo*, which shows that God is *not even indirectly* involved in tempting us to sin.

Temptation Follows a Consistent Process

> But each one is tempted when he is carried away and enticed by his own lust. Then when lust has conceived, it gives birth to sin; and when sin is accomplished, it brings forth death. (James 1:14–15)

These two verses form the crux of James's explanation of temptation. It is the only place in all the Bible where the process of allurement is clearly expounded. Here's how it happens.

First, *the bait is dropped*. We can be hooked by temptation like a fish by a worm because we're hungry—hungry for the fulfillment of our physical and spiritual needs. God promises to provide for these needs, but Satan also knows about our hungers. And although he cannot force us to partake, he is a skilled angler, knowing when, where, and how to drop bait that might lure us away from God.

Second, *our inner desire is attracted to the bait*. James wrote that "each one is carried away and enticed," implying subtle persuasion rather than forced submission. The Greek word used for *enticed* is a fishing term, meaning, "to lure by a bait." We all know that a hook baited with clothespins won't catch many fish! To pull that

4. Curtis Vaughan, *James: A Study Guide* (Grand Rapids, Mich.: Zondervan Publishing House, 1974), pp. 29–30.

fish out from its comfortable hiding place, the bait must be attractive and interesting.

Dietrich Bonhoeffer vividly describes what happens in our hearts when our desire lunges for the bait.

> At this moment God is quite unreal to us, he loses all reality, and only desire for the creature is real; the only reality is the devil. Satan does not here fill us with hatred of God, but with forgetfulness of God. . . . The lust thus aroused envelops the mind and will of man in deepest darkness. The powers of clear discrimination and of decision are taken from us.[5]

Third, *sin occurs when we yield to temptation*. James 1:15 says, "When lust has conceived, it gives birth to sin." James uses the word *conceived* alluding to the birthing process. Just as in the physical realm two elements must be joined together to create conception, so it also follows in the moral realm. To follow our fishing analogy, when desire and bait meet and we choose to take the bait, sin occurs. Remember, temptation to choose the bait is not sin, but taking it is.

Fourth, *sin results in death*. Even though sin sometimes brings a temporary period of pleasure, it always leads to death (v. 15). James is not referring here to physical death, for then none of us would be alive. Nor is he referring to spiritual death, for then no one could be saved. The fulfillment of our lust brings about in the believer's life a death-like existence.

> Guilt creeps in on cat's paws and steals whatever joy might have flickered in our eyes. Confidence is replaced by doubt, and honesty is elbowed out by rationalization. Exit peace. Enter turmoil. Just as the pleasure of indulgence ceases, the hunger for relief begins.
>
> Our vision is shortsighted and our myopic life now has but one purpose—to find release for our guilt. Or as Paul questioned for all of us, "What a wretched man I am! Who will rescue me from this body of death?"[6]

---

5. Bonhoeffer, *Creation and Fall and Temptation*, pp. 116–117.

Temptation Flourishes on Inconsistent Thinking

Do not be deceived, my beloved brethren. (v. 16)

Literally, the word *deceived* means "to be led down the wrong path." James issues this warning in the form of a command: "Don't allow lust to blur your thinking so that you forsake the truth to follow a lie." The idea that giving in to temptation will lead to contentment is a complete fallacy and inconsistent with both Scripture and experience.

> Solomon tells us that the eyes of man are never satisfied (Proverbs 27:20). One more lustful look or one more piece of pie never satisfies. In fact, quite the opposite takes place. Every time we say yes to temptation, we make it harder to say no the next time.[7]

The battlefront for resisting being drawn away from God is in the mind. Each time we yield to temptation we believe a lie—and what's worse, we start living one too.

Focus that Determines Victory

James next turns from his in-depth look at temptation to ways of overcoming it.

Victory Comes through Dwelling on the Good

> Every good thing given and every perfect gift is from above, coming down from the Father of lights, with whom there is no variation or shifting shadow. (v. 17)

Someone once wrote, "Sow a thought and reap an action. Sow an action and reap a habit. Sow a habit and reap a character. Sow a character and reap a destiny."[8] Victory comes from dwelling on those "good things" and "perfect gifts" that God has provided for us. The apostle Paul said, "Whatever is true, whatever is honorable, whatever is right, whatever is pure, whatever is lovely, whatever is

---

6. Max Lucado, *No Wonder They Call Him the Savior* (Portland, Oreg.: Multnomah Press, 1986), p. 139.

7. Jerry Bridges, *The Pursuit of Holiness* (Colorado Springs, Colo.: NavPress, 1978), p. 95.

8. Author unknown, as quoted by Donald Grey Barnhouse in *God's Covenant, God's Discipline, God's Glory* (Grand Rapids, Mich.: William B. Eerdmans Publishing Company, 1964), vol. 4, p. 158.

of good repute, if there is any excellence and if anything worthy of praise, dwell on these things" (Phil. 4:8). If we sow these thoughts consistently, we are better able to crowd out the weeds of temptation . . . and harvest more fruit of the Spirit.

Victory Comes through Living the Truth

> In the exercise of His will He brought us forth by the word of truth, so that we would be a kind of first fruits among His creatures. (James 1:18)

God brings people to salvation through the "word of truth"— God's Word. Having trusted Him for our eternal life, we are to continue relying on His Word for deliverance in our daily struggle against temptation. In Psalm 119:9, the psalmist counsels, "How can a young man keep his way pure? / By keeping it according to Your word." And in verse 11 he says, "Your word I have treasured in my heart, that I may not sin against You."

Yet how many of us pray for deliverance from some temptation, only to turn right around and expose ourselves to it again? It has been said, "To pray against temptations, and yet to rush into occasions, is to thrust your fingers into the fire, and then pray they might not be burnt."[9] Christians cannot achieve victory over temptation with knowledge alone. We must sow God's Word into our daily living through obedience. Then temptation will begin to lose its foothold in our lives.

A Final Thought

Mark Antony's most widely known and costly temptation floated to him on a barge. Bedecked as dazzling bait, Cleopatra sailed up the Cydnus River straight into Mark Antony's unguarded heart. Their adulterous relationship, with its passing pleasures, cost him his wife, his place as a world leader, and ultimately his life.

Sow a thought . . . reap your destiny. Mark Antony wouldn't resist temptation. Will you?

---

9. Thomas Seeker, as quoted in *The New Dictionary of Thoughts*, comp. Tryon Edwards, rev. and enl. by C.N. Catrevas, Jonathan Edwards, and Ralph Emerson Browns (Standard Book Company, 1966), p. 663.

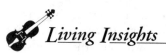 *Living Insights*

Temptation knows no limits, is no respecter of title or position, plays no favorites, ignores all human barriers, and blends into any situation. Like a powerful undertow, temptation pulls us away from God's protective shores and into the hazardous reef of sin.

What current of temptation tends to pull you out of God's harbor?

_____

_____

_____

_____

We fall into sin, not because we misunderstand temptation, but because we fail to recognize the rhythm of sin's enticing song. From this study we know a few facts about temptation: 1) temptation is always present; 2) temptation is never prompted by God; and 3) temptation flourishes on inconsistent thinking. Which of these insights is most helpful to you personally? Why?

_____

_____

_____

_____

The apostle Paul said, "No temptation has overtaken you but such as is common to man" (1 Cor. 10:13). Equally common—and tragic—are the consequences of succumbing to temptation. Scripture says that the wages of sin is death. Every sin has consequences, even if they are hard to pinpoint at the time. Carefully considering those consequences can help you resist sin's pull. What is the cost of yielding to your greatest temptation? What would you lose? Whom would you hurt?

_____

_____

_____

Now, contemplate the benefits of successfully resisting temptation. Read James 1:12. What blessings does God have for you as you keep yourself from sin?

_____

_____

According to James, we overcome temptation by dwelling on that which is good (v. 17) and by living the truth (v. 18). Accountability partners can also stand as intercessors in our struggle to overcome. Have you been able to resist temptation, particularly when sin seems most appealing? If so, what strategy has been most helpful?

_____

_____

_____

_____

Read 1 Corinthians 10:13 again. Remember that God is on your side. He is faithful and will not allow you to be tempted beyond what you are able. Keep your eyes focused on the good that comes when you resist temptation. Let God be your strength.

 Questions for Group Discussion

1. Review James 1:13–14 and 17–18 together. These verses clearly state that God is not tempted by evil, nor does He tempt anyone. Furthermore, "not only does God *not* tempt us, He is also actively providing everything good that we find in life. We are not to attribute evil intent to God—God is the source of good gifts, especially the new birth (1:18). He is the author of salvation, not temptation."[10] What do these verses reveal about the nature and character of God? What do these verses reveal about us?

10. Bruce M. Barton, David R. Veerman, and Neil Wilson, eds., *James*, Life Application Bible Commentary series; Grant Osborne, series ed. (Wheaton, Ill.: Tyndale House Publishers, Inc., 1992), p. 27.

2. James says we are "carried away and enticed" by our own *lusts*. When we hear temptation described in these terms, we often think exclusively of sexual temptation. Describe and discuss some other forms of temptation that cause us to be easily persuaded or lured away from what is best in our lives.

3. According to James 1:15, when temptation finds full expression in our lives it gives birth to sin, and "when sin is accomplished, it brings forth death." Discuss what it means to live a "death-like" existence as a consequence of sin in our lives.

4. Temptation is like a dishonest acquaintance, outwardly appealing but always hiding corrupt motives. James warns us, "Do not be deceived" (v. 16). How can we overcome temptation in our lives? How can we stop being deceived?

5. James identifies God's purpose and desire for all believers in the final verse of this passage. God brings us forth, gives birth to us, through the word of truth, in order that we might be a kind of first fruits among all He has created. What does it mean to be "a kind of first fruits among [God's] creatures?" (See Romans 8:19–23; 1 Corinthians 15:20–23; 2 Thessalonians 2:13.)

6. Close your time together by praying in groups of two or three. Pray for one another, asking God to provide the strength and determination to resist temptation this week.

Chapter 4

THE GREAT DIVORCE
James 1:19–27

Let's take some time to consider a serious subject: divorce. Not the kind that occurs between a husband and wife, but the kind that occurs in a Christian between hearing the Word and living the Word. The grounds for this type of divorce is not incompatibility but inconsistency. A. W. Tozer lamented,

> There is an evil which I have seen under the sun.
> . . . It is the glaring disparity between theology and practice among professing Christians.
> So wide is the gulf that separates theory from practice in the church that an inquiring stranger who chances upon both would scarcely dream that there was any relation between them. An intelligent observer of our human scene who heard the Sunday morning sermon and later watched the Sunday afternoon conduct of those who had heard it would conclude that he has been examining two distinct and contrary religions. . . .
> It appears that too many Christians want to enjoy the thrill of feeling right but are not willing to endure the inconvenience of being right. So the divorce between theory and practice becomes permanent in fact, though in word the union is declared to be eternal. Truth sits forsaken and grieves till her professed followers come home for a brief visit, but she sees them depart again when the bills come due.[1]

Thus far in our study, James has dealt with trials (1:1–12) and temptations (vv. 13–18). Now he comes to the basic theme behind his letter—the importance of behaving as we believe.

As we focus on verses 19–27, let's make four brief observations about the truth James presents. First, *it is imperative truth*. At first, verse 19 seems like a merely descriptive statement, "This you know,

---

1. A.W. Tozer, *The Root of the Righteous* (1955; Camp Hill, Pa.: Christian Publications, 1986), pp. 51–53.

my beloved brethren," but it ought to be taken as a command: "Know this." It's as if James is saying, "Listen up! This is important." Second, *it is family truth*. James addresses his readers as "my beloved brethren." It assumes that you know the Lord and it therefore is talking to you as a member of God's family. Third, *it is personal truth*. "Everyone must be quick to hear, slow to speak and slow to anger." The truth is addressed to each believer in the Christian family. Fourth, *it is logical truth*. James carries his thoughts through a logical progression that involves (1) preparing ourselves for the truth, (2) actually taking in the truth, and (3) responding correctly to that truth in our daily lives.

Preparing Ourselves for the Truth

Anyone who has ever painted a house knows that the hardest work is preparing the surface, not the actual painting. This is true in any endeavor, and for good reason. The better the preparation, the better and more lasting the results. As in painting, preparation is necessary also for receiving truth. Without preparation, we simply whitewash our lives with knowledge that will quickly peel, revealing an unchanged character underneath.

James had seen too many Christians who tried to slap on God's truth without properly preparing themselves so that it would stick. So beginning in verse 19, he sets forth four requisites for preparing ourselves to receive God's truth.

An Open Ear

The first essential is an open ear.

> This you know, my beloved brethren. But everyone
> must be quick to hear. (v. 19a)

One reason our lives are often divorced from the truth is because we don't really hear what God says. The problem isn't that we're hard of hearing, it's that we're hard of *listening*. Jesus constantly rebuked the Pharisees for this very problem with the stinging question, "Have you not heard?" The obvious answer, of course, was yes, they had heard God's Word. The Pharisees were known for their meticulous knowledge of the Law. But they didn't really listen to what they heard. They didn't allow God's truth to speak to them personally, individually.

A Controlled Tongue

Second, James says,

> Everyone must be . . . slow to speak. (v. 19)

A young man once approached Socrates to ask if the philosopher would teach him the gift of oratory. His request was then followed by an incessant stream of words until, finally, Socrates placed his hand over the inquirer's mouth and said, "Young man, I will have to charge you a double fee." When the fellow asked why, Socrates said, "I will have to teach you two sciences. First, how to hold your tongue, and then, how to use it wisely."[2]

No one can speak and learn at the same time. How much time do you spend in silence preparing yourself for the sowing of God's Word? Before we can listen, we must first learn to control our tongues.

A Calm Spirit

Third, James says,

> Everyone must be . . . slow to anger. (v. 19)

Why?

> For the anger of man does not achieve the righteousness of God. (v. 20)

Like weeds, anger sprouts quickly and chokes out the faith that pleases God. We can be so preoccupied with spiteful thinking that we have no room for thoughts of God, nor energy for godly deeds. Anger demands our full attention. Being slow to anger means keeping anger in check, dealing with anger before it deals with us, and being patient with others.

A Clean Heart

The final step of preparation is a clean heart. To achieve that, James says we must do two things.

> [Put] aside all filthiness and all that remains of wickedness. (v. 21a)

---

2. Spiros Zodhiates, *The Behavior of Belief* (Grand Rapids, Mich.: William B. Eerdmans Publishing Co., 1959), p. 94.

First, there must be the removal of "filthiness." William Barclay explains that the word *filthiness* is a vivid term derived from the Greek word *rupos*.

> When *rupos* is used in a medical sense, it means *wax in the ear*. It is just possible that it still retains that meaning here; and that James is telling his readers to get rid of everything which would stop their ears to the true word of God. When wax gathers in the ear, it can make a man deaf; and a man's sins can make him deaf to God.[3]

Second, in addition to ridding ourselves of obvious "filthiness," we're also to put aside "all that remains of wickedness." The Greek term for *wickedness* refers to hidden sins, motives, and attitudes that cause the corrupt outer behavior that others see.

Taking in the Truth

James has shown us how to prepare ourselves for the truth. He now provides us with two important insights into the process of actually *receiving* truth.

> In humility receive the word implanted, which is able to save your souls. (v. 21b)

One essential ingredient for receiving truth is having the right attitude. James wants our attitude to reflect humility, which means "with gentleness, openness; having a teachable spirit." With this, he says there must also be an action—we must receive, meaning we need to welcome it. So, whenever truth knocks, we're to open the door and welcome it with great hospitality.

Responding to the Truth

Many Christians live divorced from truth because they confuse agreeing with Scripture with obeying it. James, however, urges us to go beyond preparing and receiving; we must also act on what we've heard.

---

3. William Barclay, *The Letters of James and Peter*, rev. ed., The Daily Study Bible series (Philadelphia, Pa.: The Westminster Press, 1976), p. 57.

The Command

> But prove yourselves doers of the word, and not
> merely hearers who delude themselves. (v. 22)

Notice James doesn't say *just* be doers. God isn't looking for
activists who don't know His Word. Nor is He interested in hearers
who know His Word but do nothing. The Greek term for *hearers*
is an interesting one. It refers to someone who audits a course at a
university—someone who listens carefully and takes notes, but has
no assignments, tests, or responsibilities. In short, it represents
someone who merely takes in information.

James plainly states that those who simply audit the faith are
deceiving themselves about their Christianity, and that sincere
believers will prove their authenticity by applying what they hear.

The Illustration

James describes two different types of people: the hearer and
the doer.

> For if anyone is a hearer of the word and not a doer,
> he is like a man who looks at his natural face in a
> mirror; for once he has looked at himself and gone
> away, he has immediately forgotten what kind of
> person he was. But one who looks intently at the
> perfect law, the law of liberty, and abides by it, not
> having become a forgetful hearer but an effectual
> doer, this man will be blessed in what he does.
> (vv. 23–25)

In this classic metaphor, God's Word is compared to a mirror.
But unlike a physical mirror, which only reflects outward appearance,
Scripture reveals our inner character. The hearer James describes
promptly forgets what both reflect; while the effectual doer, on the
other hand, gives careful attention to the Scriptures, responds
positively, applies what is heard, and is genuinely fulfilled.

The Application

The effectual doer obeys what the Scriptures reveal and, in turn,
becomes a mirror reflecting real Christianity. How can we know
when someone is an effectual doer? James provides three indications.

First, *there is no divorce between the truth and the tongue.*

> If anyone thinks himself to be religious, and yet does not bridle his tongue but deceives his own heart, this man's religion is worthless. (v. 26)

Second, *there is no divorce between the truth and the needs of others.*

> Pure and undefiled religion in the sight of our God and Father is this: to visit orphans and widows in their distress . . . (v. 27a)

Third, *there is no divorce between the truth and our Christian uniqueness in a fallen world.*

> . . . and to keep oneself unstained by the world. (v. 27b)

Is your life on the rocks because you've allowed truth and practice to drift apart? Have your mind and will become estranged from one another? If so, it's time to start reconciling the two. You can begin by taking James' counsel to heart . . . *prepare, receive,* and *apply.*

Living Insights

A.W. Tozer points out the great divorce between the theology and practice among Christians when he writes, "It appears that too many Christians want to enjoy the thrill of feeling right but are not willing to endure the inconvenience of being right."[4]

Have you experienced times in your spiritual life when your theology and practice were in conflict? In what ways did you behave differently than you believed?

_____

_____

Why is it difficult to act according to what the Bible teaches and what we profess to believe?

_____

_____

4. A.W. Tozer, *The Root of the Righteous*, pp. 51–53.

How can you maintain consistency between what you know about God's Word and what you do in response?

_____

_____

_____

James instructs us to be, first, "quick to hear;" second, "slow to speak;" and third, "slow to anger" (v. 19). Which of these commands do you find most challenging in your personal relationships? Have you changed your behavior in order to overcome this weakness? If so, how?

_____

_____

_____

When we reconcile the divorce between truth and action, we become receptive to the Word and its impact on our daily lives. The New International Version translates James 1:22 as follows:

> Do not merely listen to the word, and so deceive yourselves. Do what it says.

What is one thing you can do today to be a doer and not merely a hearer of God's word?

_____

_____

 ## Questions for Group Discussion

Developing a faith "unstained by the world" (v. 27) requires action. We can't simply hear the Word; we must do something in response. Getting beyond the general trials and temptations of life, we are now challenged to confront our behavior—what we do in response to what we hear. Inconsistent faith, like a discordant marriage, leads to disastrous consequences. James offers counsel that helps bridge the great divide between what we believe and what we do.

1. First, we are to prepare ourselves for the truth. With an open ear, a controlled tongue, a calm spirit, and a clean heart, we are instructed to humbly receive the Word, which is able to save our souls (vv. 19–21). How are we to be quick to hear, slow to speak, and slow to anger? How can we "put aside all filthiness and all that remains of wickedness"? What are the consequences of failing to prepare for God's truth?

2. Our attitude reflects a gentle, open, teachable spirit when we receive the truth of God's Word with humility (v. 21b). James indicates that God's Word is "implanted" within us, cultivated into the soil of our souls. What attitudes are present when you are confronted with the truth of God's Word? Have you ever felt resentful of those who speak the truth, even in love? What is the promise offered to those who welcome God's truth into their lives?

3. James commands us to "be doers, not just hearers" of the word. Our response doesn't stop with hearing; we must act upon what we hear. We are not to be auditors of the class; we're to participate in every assignment, sit for every exam, and write the graduate thesis. Define the characteristics of someone who is simply auditing the course of Christianity. Contrast these characteristics with those of someone whose life is significantly changed as a result of their Christian walk. How would you characterize yourself?

4. The forgetful man with the mirror (vv. 23–24) is caught in a trap, hearing the Word and never allowing it to penetrate below the surface—never allowing his life to be impacted by God's truth. James incites us to become effective doers of God's Word by examining the Scriptures and being obedient to its commands. How can you escape the trap and go deeper in your relationship with God? How does it feel to become vulnerable to change? What can the members of your group do to help you break through to a more meaningful relationship with God?

Chapter 5

PREJUDICE IS A SIN

James 2:1–13

Several years ago, a young, single attorney worked for a boss who gave each of his employees an annual Thanksgiving turkey. One year, before the birds were handed out, the attorney's mischievous friends replaced his real turkey with one made of papier-mâché. They carefully wrapped the bogus bird in brown paper, weighted it with lead, and even added a real turkey neck and tail to make it look and feel genuine. The day before Thanksgiving, the attorney went to the company boardroom, picked up his assigned turkey, and thanked his boss for his job and the bird.

On the bus ride home, the young man wondered what in the world to do with the big turkey in his lap. He didn't know how to cook it and couldn't possibly eat it all by himself. Before long, a discouraged-looking man got on the bus and headed towards the only vacant seat, the one next to our attorney friend. He sat down, and as they talked the young man learned that the stranger had spent the entire day job hunting with no luck. He had a large family and wondered what he would do about Thanksgiving the next day.

Suddenly the attorney was struck with a brilliant idea: *This is my day for a good deed. I'll give him my turkey!* The fellow didn't look like he'd accept charity, so the attorney asked, "How much money do you have?" "Oh, a couple of dollars and a few cents," the man answered. "Sold!" said the attorney as he put the turkey in the stranger's lap. The man was moved to tears, thrilled that his family would have a turkey for Thanksgiving. He got off the bus and waved good-bye to the attorney.

The next Monday, the attorney's friends were dying to know about the turkey. You can imagine their dismay and the young attorney's horror when they both learned what each had done. For a week, the attorney and his co-workers rode the bus searching for the stranger they had unintentionally wronged, but they never found him.[1]

You can imagine how bad the attorney must have felt. But what about the stranger? Can you imagine what he thought, how he must have felt when he discovered the turkey was only a glob of paper?

1. Charles R. Swindoll, *Three Steps Forward, Two Steps Back*, rev. ed. (Nashville, Tenn.: Thomas Nelson Publishers, 1990), pp. 23–25.

For all he knew, that young man had intentionally sold him a fake. Was he right? No. But the circumstantial evidence seemed to indicate that he was, and it would have been hard to convince him otherwise.

Like one of Aesop's fables, there's a moral behind this story: *It's impossible to judge another person's motives simply on the basis of outward appearance or any other external factor.* No one can determine the heart of another from the outside. That's why James says in chapter 2, verses 1–13, that prejudice and partiality are wrong!

The Principle Stated

James presents his case against prejudice in a tightly constructed passage. First, he introduces a principle in verse 1, then he illustrates it in verses 2–4, explains it in verses 5–11 and, finally, applies it in verses 12–13. Let's listen now as James makes his opening statement.

> My brethren, do not hold your faith in our glorious Lord Jesus Christ with an attitude of personal favoritism. (v. 1)

Clearly stated, James's point is that faith in Christ and partiality are incompatible. The word *favoritism* used here comes from two words in the Greek which, when put together, mean "to receive by face."[2] It's the idea of judging others solely on external face values, such as clothes, cars, or skin color.

It's important to note that James is not condemning the kind of discernment that comes from a thorough understanding of another's character. What he is dealing with here is our tendency to be prejudiced toward others; showing partiality because of superficial judgments based on outward appearances.

The Principle Illustrated

Following the statement of his principle, James fleshes out the issue with a vivid illustration.

The Setting

> For if a man comes into your assembly with a gold ring and dressed in fine clothes, and there also comes in a poor man in dirty clothes . . . (v. 2)

2. The same term for *favoritism* used here is found in only three other places in the New Testament. In each passage, we're assured that the Father is not a respecter of persons. When He judges, He judges the heart, not outward appearances.

Imagine, James says, you're the usher at a worship service and in comes Mr. Have followed by Mr. Have-Not. The former is adorned in gold rings and fine fabrics studded with jewels, while the latter wears ragged hand-me-downs caked with dirt. What will you do?

The Response

> . . . and you pay special attention to the one who is wearing the fine clothes, and say, "You sit here in a good place," and you say to the poor man, "You stand over there, or sit down by my footstool" . . . (v. 3)

Now, if we escorted one man down front because he's rich and sent the second to a back corner because he's poor, wouldn't our motive be something less than pure?

The Motive

> . . . have you not made distinctions among yourselves, and become judges with evil motives? (v. 4)

Two things are clarified in this verse. First, *what was done:* the usher "made distinctions." He discriminated based on appearances, exalting one and mistreating another. Second, *we're told why it was done:* because of evil motives . . . catering to the rich in hopes of selfish gain, or to maintain class distinctions, or simply out of pride and contempt.

The Principle Explained

Next, James presents three reasons why prejudice is wrong. The first reason he gives is theological: *Prejudice is inconsistent with God's methods.*

> Listen, my beloved brethren: did not God choose the poor of this world to be rich in faith and heirs of the kingdom which He promised to those who love Him? (v. 5)

Is James saying that God is partial toward the financially poor? No, of course not. As William Barclay has noted, "The great characteristic of God is his complete impartiality."[3]

3. William Barclay, *The Letters of James and Peter*, rev. ed., The Daily Study Bible series (Philadelphia, Pa.: Westminster Press, 1976), p. 63.

Barclay goes on to explain,

> James is not shutting the door on the rich—far from that. He is saying that the gospel of Christ is specially dear to the poor and that in it there is a welcome for the man who has none to welcome him, and that through it there is a value set on the man whom the world regards as valueless.[4]

James is simply saying that, from God's perspective, the real issue is the condition of one's soul. God bases His choices on the heart, not the wallet.

The apostle Paul echoes James's point in 1 Corinthians 1:25–29.

> The foolishness of God is wiser than men, and the weakness of God is stronger than men.
>
> For consider your calling, brethren, that there were not many wise according to the flesh, not many mighty, not many noble; but God has chosen the foolish things of the world to shame the wise, and God has chosen the weak things of the world to shame the things which are strong, and the base things of the world and the despised God has chosen, the things that are not, so that He might nullify the things that are, so that no man may boast before God.

James's second reason that prejudice is wrong is a logical one: *Prejudice ignores the universality of sin.*

> But you have dishonored the poor man. Is it not the rich who oppress you and personally drag you into court? Do they not blaspheme the fair name by which you have been called? (James 2:6–7)

Besides the fact that it was ludicrous to exalt the very people who persecuted them, James reminds his readers that by catering to the rich, they were denying that the wealthy are sinners and need the grace of God like all the rest.

James's last reason rests on the authority of the Bible: *Prejudice is sinful because it is inconsistent with Scripture.*

---

4. Barclay, *Letters of James and Peter*, p. 67.

If, however, you are fulfilling the royal law according to the Scripture, "You shall love your neighbor as yourself," you are doing well. But if you show partiality, you are committing sin and are convicted by the law as transgressors. (vv. 8–9)

Centuries before, Moses said in Leviticus 19:18, "You shall love your neighbor as yourself." That was God's law then, and it still is today. But if you show partiality, then you have sinned and become a lawbreaker. As one commentator observed,

Anyone who shows favoritism breaks the supreme law of love for his neighbor, the law that comprehends all laws governing one's relationships to one's fellowmen.[5]

Wouldn't it be nice if all our relationships were guided by the royal law of love? But the fact is, we all have certain built-in prejudices that influence our reactions to people. Some hold prejudices against divorced people or people who have been emotionally disabled; others against those who belong to a different political, ethnic, or religious background.

These kinds of prejudices produce cliques, gossip mongers, legalists, and power-hungry groups in churches who put enormous pressure on others to conform to their rules of behavior. Each group has its own unwritten royal law that states, "We'll love you if you don't speak with an accent . . . if you dress in a certain way . . . if you're educated . . . if . . . if . . . if . . ." The list is endless.

Now for some of us, James's condemnation of prejudice may seem a little too harsh. We think, "Sure, our love may have a few limitations, but it's not like we're murderers or anything!" James knew some would react this way, so he wrote the following. Listen.

For whoever keeps the whole law and yet stumbles in one point, he has become guilty of all. For He who said, "Do not commit adultery," also said, "Do not commit murder." Now if you do not commit adultery, but do commit murder, you have become a transgressor of the law. (James 2:10–11)

5. Donald W. Burdick, "James," in The Expositor's Bible Commentary, ed. Frank E. Gaebelein (Grand Rapids, Mich.: Zondervan Publishing House, Regency Reference Library, 1981), vol. 12, p. 180.

While it's true that some sins are more heinous than others, it is not true that we're any less guilty of breaking God's law simply because we only show partiality instead of committing murder.

The Principle Applied

In verses 12–13 James brings his thoughts on prejudice to a close with three basic principles for us to apply.

First, *let the Scriptures—not your heritage—be your standard.*

> So speak and so act as those who are to be judged
> by the law of liberty. (v. 12)

Instead of excusing your prejudices with statements like, "That's the way I was brought up," or, "That's just the way I am," allow God to change how you think, speak, and act by living according to His Word.

Second, *let love be your law.* Some of the neediest people typically receive the worst kinds of prejudiced responses. Before you respond to someone, first think, "How can I love this person? What's needed to help build this person up?"

Third, *let mercy be your message.*

> For judgment will be merciless to one who has shown
> no mercy; mercy triumphs over judgment. (v. 13)

The individual who is motivated by the law of love will exude mercy in his or her relationships.

How would you respond if you suddenly discovered that your closest friend had a background like the woman at the well or the apostle Paul?[6] Would it change your love? Probably not. Then why are we so quick to condemn others with similar backgrounds whom we hardly even know? The reason, James says, is prejudice.

Unlike an Aesop fable, our lives are real stories that are constantly read by the people around us. What will be the moral behind your story? The law of love or the sin of prejudice?

---

6. See John 4:5–18 and Acts 7:58–8:3.

 *Living Insights*

Prejudice often hides behind a veil of respectability. To safeguard our testimony, we may avoid contact with certain undesirable people. To widen our network, we may "buddy up" to the "right" people. To grow our ministry, we may give special treatment to those who really can make things happen. All for good reasons, on the surface. Underneath, though, is a pool of prejudice, bubbling into our attitudes.

Ask God to reveal areas of "personal favoritism" in your own life. Where have you seen evidence of an attitude of "partiality" in your community? In your church? In your personal life?

_____

_____

_____

Our hectic lifestyles cause us to make snap judgments about people we encounter throughout the day. What criteria do you use to evaluate the people you meet? What criteria are they using to measure you? What criteria does God use to measure us all?

_____

_____

_____

James isn't telling us we can't make meaningful distinctions between people. He is challenging us to examine the motives behind our distinctions. Evil motives produce prejudice. Self-oriented motives lead to attitudes of favoritism, partiality, and prejudice. Others-oriented motives lead to positive distinctions based on character and heart—something easily measured by God but elusive for us. What can you do to ensure that the distinctions you make are not based upon prejudice but according to godly discernment?

_____

_____

_____

Questions for Group Discussion

Our English word *prejudice* stems from a Latin noun that emphasizes a prejudgment of someone, causing us to form an opinion without knowing the facts. Once we've raced to our conclusions, based on incomplete facts, we're well on our way to irrational thinking—thinking that results in an insidious attitude that says, "Don't bother me with the truth, my mind is made up." The whole point of James 2:1–13 is to diffuse this kind of faulty thinking.

1. As a group, read through the text once more and probe the spirit of prejudice. Discuss the reasons why prejudice causes the following to clash head-on:
    a) Faith and favoritism (v. 1)
    b) The wealthy and the poor (vv. 2–7)
    c) Self and neighbor (vv. 8–11)
    d) Mercy and judgment (vv. 12–13)

2. Examples of prejudice surround our lives every day. Discuss how members of the group are impacted by personal, corporate, and institutional prejudice. How does an attitude of "personal favoritism" or "partiality" demonstrate itself in your daily life?

3. James presents three reasons why prejudice is wrong: *prejudice is inconsistent with God's methods; prejudice ignores the universality of sin;* and *prejudice is inconsistent with Scripture.* Which of these scriptural principles has the most influence on your thinking? Why?

4. Individual bias remains hidden by our culture of political correctness. It is easy to hide our prejudice among carefully considered public personas and well-chosen words. But God knows the condition of our hearts. As appropriate, share with the group areas where you are feeling particularly challenged by this passage. With an attitude of sincere confession, disclose those areas where you have been guilty of favoritism, partiality, or prejudice. Pause to pray with each member of the group who chooses to reveal their personal struggle in this area.

5. How can we help struggling co-workers, friends, and family recognize the impact of personal prejudice on their relationships with others? With the Lord?

6. Close with prayer—asking the Lord to reveal areas of personal prejudice, to strengthen our resolve to examine the heart rather than externals, and to provide the courage to stand against prejudice in any form.

Chapter 6

YOU CAN'T HAVE ONE
WITHOUT THE OTHER

James 2:14–26

Someone once said that faith is like calories: you can't see them, but you can always see their results! That is the major theme resonating throughout James's letter—*results*. Faith produces works. And nowhere is this theme more passionately argued than in James 2:14–26.

Initial Clarification

As we begin our study, let's clarify one critical issue. That is the apparent contradiction between the thrust of our passage today—"a man is justified by works and not by faith alone" (2:24)—and Paul's great thesis in Romans 3–5: "a man is justified by faith apart from works of the Law" (Rom. 3:28; see also Eph. 2:8–9; 2 Tim. 1:9; Titus 3:5).

It was this same issue that caused Martin Luther to label James a "right strawy epistle,"[1] meaning that he felt it lacked solid, biblical doctrine. To Luther, whose battle cry in the Reformation was "justification by faith alone," James's emphasis on justification by works was blatant heresy. But are Paul and James really in contradiction? To find out, let's examine three important differences between them.

First, it's important to understand that the *emphasis* of Paul's and James's writings are different. Paul stresses the root of salvation, which is faith in Christ plus nothing. James calls attention to the fruit *after* salvation. Every believer rooted in Christ by faith will bear fruit, like branches on a vine (see John 15:4–5). Paul talks about the root; James talks about the fruit.

A second contrast between Paul and James is *perspective*. Paul looks at life from God's perspective, while James looks at life from a human perspective. Paul sees the fire in the fireplace, while James eyes the smoke coming out the chimney. To James, the world should

---

1. Quoted by J. Ronald Blue, "James," in *The Bible Knowledge Commentary*, New Testament ed., eds. John F. Walvoord and Roy B. Zuck (Wheaton, Ill.: SP Publications, Victor Books, 1983), p. 815.

be able to tell that a faith burns in our hearts by the works they see coming out in our lives.

The third contrast, and perhaps the most important one, is the difference in *terms*. Both Paul and James use the same word, *justified*, but with two different meanings. When Paul mentions justification, he means the act of God at salvation whereby He declares the believing sinner righteous while still in a sinning state. James, on the other hand, uses it to mean *validation* or *evidence*. We justify or prove our faith, James says, by our works.

Perhaps commentator W. H. Griffith Thomas reconciled these two ideas best when he wrote,

> It has been well said that St. Paul and St. James are not soldiers of different armies fighting against each other, but soldiers of the same army fighting back to back against enemies coming from opposite directions.[2]

James strawy? No. If understood properly, James's letter is as solidly biblical and practical as they come.

Expositional Study

Our passage today is also as feisty as they come in the New Testament. James has a bone to pick—one that he has been building up to since he opened his letter and that he will continue to underscore until he closes.

Introductory Question

To introduce the cardinal passage of his letter, James asks two rhetorical questions that not only beg an answer but also an analysis.

> What use is it, my brethren, if someone says he has faith but he has no works? (2:14a)

What good does it do, asks James, to say you have faith if you have no works to justify that claim? It's like asking, "What good is it to have a driver's license if you don't drive?" Answer? None. So what good is a faith that doesn't produce works? You guessed it. After pointing out the worthlessness of a workless faith, James then asks an even deeper question, "Can that faith save him?" (v. 14b).

2. W. H. Griffith Thomas, *St. Paul's Epistle to the Romans: A Devotional Commentary* (Grand Rapids, Mich.: William B. Eerdmans Publishing Co., 1947), vol. 1, p. 132.

In Greek, questions can be framed in two different ways. One phrasing expects a positive answer, and the other, like James's second question, expects a negative answer. Essentially, he's asking, "Can that empty claim of faith save?" And the answer, of course, is no. The great leaders of the Reformation used to say we are justified by faith alone, but not by the faith which is alone. Faith is accompanied by fruit; it is not found in hollow words.

Characteristics of Genuine Faith

Next, in verses 15–20, James illustrates four marks of faith. First, *faith is not indifferent . . . but involved.*

> If a brother or sister is without clothing and in need of daily food, and one of you says to them, "Go in peace, be warmed and be filled," and yet you do not give them what is necessary for their body, what use is that? (vv. 15–16)

This illustration is easy to understand because, in one way or another, most of us have been that needy person and can still remember the empty platitudes we received instead of real help. One paraphrase renders the emotionally detached, dispassionate response in verse 16 this way:

> Keep up your spirits, don't become discouraged; someone will yet come to your relief; go away from my presence comforted.[3]

What is missing? James says it's the proof of faith—real food and real clothes. No one echoes this point better than the apostle John.

> But whoever has the world's goods, and sees his brother in need and closes his heart against him, how does the love of God abide in him? Little children, let us not love with word or with tongue, but in deed and truth. (1 John 3:17–18)

Second, *faith is not independent . . . but in partnership.*

> Even so faith, if it has no works, is dead, being by itself. (James 2:17)

---

3. Curtis Vaughan, *James: A Study Guide* (Grand Rapids, Mich.: Zondervan Publishing House, 1969), p. 61.

There was a song made popular years ago titled "Love and Marriage." Remember the beginning? "Love and marriage, love and marriage, go together like a horse and carriage." Its final stanza concluded with the words, "You can't have one without the other."[4] Faith and works go together like a horse and carriage. You can't have one without the other. Dissolve the partnership and faith dies. Faith was never designed to dwell alone, separate from the partner that proves its existence.

Third, *faith is not invisible . . . but on display.* James illustrates this by creating an imaginary conversation between two people. The one speaking in verse 18 agrees with James.

> But someone may well say, "You have faith, and
> I have works; show me your faith without the works,
> and I will show you my faith by my works." (v. 18)

The word *show* means to bring to light, to display or exhibit. James's imaginary friend is talking about demonstrating faith. "Do your best to show me your faith without using works, and I'll demonstrate my faith by my works. We'll see which one of us really has faith."

Some might argue, however, "Look, there are all kinds of Christians. Some have the gift of works, others are quiet, never displaying their faith." But that's like saying some people have the gift of breathing and others don't! We delude ourselves if we think it doesn't matter whether we evidence our faith or not. James's whole point is that if it doesn't show, you don't have it.

Fourth, *faith is not merely intellectual . . . but from the heart.* Next James picks on the other imaginary partner in the conversation, someone we might call a religious intellectual—like the priests and Pharisees in Jesus' day (see Luke 10:25-37).

> You believe that God is one. (v. 19a)

This person's defense against not having any works is to hide behind an impressive knowledge of God's Word. "My theology is impeccable; I believe God is One, just like it says in Deuteronomy 6:4." "Wonderful," James says, "join hands with the demons."

> You do well; the demons also believe, and shudder.
> (v. 19b)

---

4. Sammy Cahn, "Love and Marriage," as quoted in *Songs with Lyrics* by Sammy Cahn (Ft. Lauderdale, Fla.: Cahn Music Co., 1955).

The demons have their religious facts straight, but they're still demons. Like the Pharisees, we can know all the religious facts we want, but until we recognize our need for Christ and place our trust in Him, we're no more Christian than the demons.

There is one interesting difference between our intellectual friend and the demons, however. James says that the demonic tribes tremble at the thought of God. The Greek term used for *shudder* suggests a "rough, uneven surface." They get goose bumps! But the dead faith of the religious intellectual doesn't produce even that much of a reaction.

James is not ridiculing intelligent faith; rather, he's mocking those religious intellectuals who love to debate religious truth but have no plans whatsoever to commit themselves to following Jesus Christ.

Next, James invites his imaginary intellectual to learn a hard fact about the religious show that he calls faith.

> But are you willing to recognize, you foolish fellow,
> that faith without works is useless? (v. 20)

If you take away the element of application, you're left only with mere intellectual assent, which neither glorifies God nor helps the person who possesses it.

Examples of Faith

To emphasize that faith is evidenced by good works, James now directs our attention to Abraham and Rahab.

> Was not Abraham our father justified by works when he offered up Isaac his son on the altar? You see that faith was working with his works, and as a result of the works, faith was perfected; and the Scripture was fulfilled which says, "And Abraham believed God, and it was reckoned to him as righteousness," and he was called the friend of God. You see that a man is justified by works and not by faith alone. In the same way, was not Rahab the harlot also justified by works when she received the messengers and sent them out by another way? (vv. 21–25)

James couldn't have picked two more opposite people as proof that our works prove our faith. Abraham was the father of the Jews; Rahab was a pagan prostitute. Abraham was a moral, admired Jewish patriarch; Rahab was a harlot who was looked upon with disdain and considered insignificant. Yet both evidenced the same kind of faith. Abraham "justified" (proved) his faith by offering up his son Isaac (see Gen. 22), and Rahab demonstrated her faith when she risked her life to protect two Israelite spies (see Josh. 2).

Concluding Principle

Finally, James summarizes his entire discussion in verse 26.

> For just as the body without the spirit is dead, so also faith without works is dead.

The concluding principle is simple. When there is separation, there is death. It's true physically, when the soul separates from the body; and it's true spiritually, when faith is separated from works. Without works, faith is nothing but a corpse, void of vitality and useless to everybody but the undertaker.

Faith, like calories, cannot be seen, but James says that you can always see its results. What results do others see in your life? Take a moment to think back over the characteristics of faith and compare them to your own.

Faith is involved . . . is yours? Faith is a partnership . . . is yours? Faith is displayed . . . is yours? Faith is from the heart . . . is yours?

Remember, James isn't saying that our salvation is dependent on our works. Nor is he trying to make us produce more works out of guilt or fear. He's only questioning those who say they are Christians but whose lives never show any evidence of that claim. "If you say that you're saved, why doesn't your life show it?" It's a fair question and a penetrating one.

Living Insights

Have you been putting on weight lately, spiritually speaking? In contrast to our physical bodies, our souls are always better off gaining weight than losing it. As Solomon noted,

> The soul of the sluggard craves and gets nothing,
> But the soul of the diligent is made fat.
> (Proverbs 13:4)

Use this time to count the calories of your faith. On a scale of one to ten, one being malnourished and ten being well-fed, rate how well you are evidencing the genuine characteristics of faith.

Faith is not indifferent but involved.

1   2   3   4   5   6   7   8   9   10

Faith is not independent but in partnership.

1   2   3   4   5   6   7   8   9   10

Faith is not invisible but on display.

1   2   3   4   5   6   7   8   9   10

Faith is not intellectual but from the heart.

1   2   3   4   5   6   7   8   9   10

Which of these areas needs some fattening up in your life?

_____

_____

_____

With this area in mind, take a moment now to begin developing a new diet for your soul. How can you provide the healthy nutrients it needs? *Bon appétit!*

_____

_____

_____

Questions for Group Discussion

One commentator explains the faith/works dilemma concisely:

> We are not saved *by* deeds; we are saved *for* deeds; these are the twin truths of the Christian life. Paul's emphasis is on the first and James's is on the second. In fact they do not contradict but complement each

other; and the message of both is essential to the Christian faith in its fullest form.[5]

1. Our friends often struggle between knowing about God and truly accepting Christ with a heart-felt faith. What is the difference between a professing faith and a genuine faith in Christ?

2. "The one thing that James cannot stand is profession without practice, words without deeds."[6] He tells us, "faith, if it has no works, is dead, being by itself" (v. 17). In other words, genuine faith doesn't exist alone; it exists in partnership with works. Discuss how our actions reflect our faith in Christ. In what ways can we expect our actions (thoughts, behaviors, motives) to change after we come to know the Lord?

3. James illustrates genuine faith as evidenced by Abraham and Rahab. How does Abraham demonstrate his faith in God in Genesis 22:1–12? How does Rahab demonstrate her faith in Joshua 2:1–15? In what way does the evidence of their faith reveal the condition of their hearts?

4. We may never be called to sacrifice as much as Abraham and Rahab in order to demonstrate our faith in God. However, we will probably be challenged to let go of something important. What are you willing to risk losing in order to demonstrate your faith in God? How about your financial security? Your lifestyle? Your possessions? Share with the group those areas in your life that would be most difficult to sacrifice to God.

5. Our salvation is not dependent on our works, yet our good works are evidence of our salvation. Some people remain undecided about their relationship with Christ yet manage to live a good and moral life. Are these good deeds sufficient? What is necessary in order to ensure an eternal life with Christ?

6. Pray for those in your group who are still working through these decisions, for family members and friends who struggle to understand the relationship between faith and works.

5. William Barclay, *The Letters of James and Peter*, rev. ed., The Daily Study Bible series (Philadelphia, Pa.: Westminster Press, 1976), p. 74.

6. Barclay, *Letters of James and Peter*, p. 75.

Chapter 7

BRIDLING THE BEAST IN YOUR BODY

James 3:1–12

C an you name the muscle in the human body that is exercised the most, yet controlled the least?

Medically, it's only a two-ounce slab of muscle, mucous membrane, and nerves that enable us to chew, taste, swallow food, and articulate words. Relationally, it's a beast.

It can frame deceit (Ps. 50:19), devise destruction (Ps. 52:2), devour (Ps. 52:4), be a sharp sword (Ps. 57:4), backbite (Prov. 25:23), flatter (Prov. 28:23), and poison (Rom. 3:13).

You know this protean lump simply as the *tongue*.

It's the often beastly nature of the tongue that James lashes with his pen in today's passage. But is it our literal tongues that are the real problem? No. In Matthew 15, Jesus unmasks the culprit that controls the tongue.

> After Jesus called the crowd to Him, He said to them, "Hear, and understand. It is not what enters into the mouth that defiles the man, but what proceeds out of the mouth, this defiles the man. . . . Do you not understand that everything that goes into the mouth passes into the stomach, and is eliminated? But the things that proceed out of the mouth come from the heart, and those defile the man. For out of the heart come evil thoughts, murders, adulteries, fornications, thefts, false witness, slanders." (vv. 10–11, 17–19)

The tongue is neither friend nor foe. It's merely a messenger that delivers the dictates of the heart. So every time James uses the word *tongue* in our passage today, think *heart*.

Look closely now as James peers with the Great Physician's light at the tongue and teaches us about our hearts.

Introduction

James begins his examination with a surprising command.

Command

> Let not many of you become teachers, my brethren, knowing that as such we will incur a stricter judgment. (James 3:1)

Is James condemning the teaching ministry? No. Actually, he's warning against clamoring for the position without carefully weighing the cost. It is important to understand that teachers will be judged more strictly than most. Why? Because they're responsible for teaching truth—God's truth—not their own opinions. Because the words teachers sow will affect many lives. And because teachers are expected to model the truth they teach. James explained it this way.

Explanation

> For we all stumble in many ways. If anyone does not stumble in what he says, he is a perfect man, able to bridle the whole body as well. (v. 2)

This especially applies to teachers. Since no one is infallible, and since the tongue is the tool of the teaching trade, teachers must master the use of this tool to avoid stumbling into "a stricter judgment."

Clarification

Before we move deeper into our passage, let's pause to be sure we understand two important points. First, James is not condemning teaching; he's only warning against rushing into it without weighing the responsibility. And second, James is not promoting silence; he's proposing control.

Exposition

In verses 3–5, James emphasizes the power of the tongue through the use of three illustrations.

The Tongue: Small but Powerful

> Now if we put the bits into the horses' mouths so that they will obey us, we direct their entire body as well. (v. 3)

With the length of a rope or a few strips of leather and a small piece of metal in a horse's mouth, a rider can control the horse's whole body. In the same way, James says, the tongue is a bit—a small, two-ounce bit nestled in our mouths that controls the direction of our lives.

Next, James likens the tongue to a rudder, something proportionately smaller than the bit when compared to the size of the ships it guides.

> Look at the ships also, though they are so great and are driven by strong winds, are still directed by a very small rudder wherever the inclination of the pilot desires. (v. 4)

Through the centuries, as ships have grown larger and heavier, James's illustration has grown more poignant than he could possibly have imagined. Yet, despite the fact that our floating behemoths could swallow whole the vessels of James's day, they still have their course determined by a comparatively small wedge of metal called a rudder. The rudder of the human body is that small slab of muscle called the tongue.

Horses, ships, and now James's third and most extreme analogy: fire.

> So also the tongue is a small part of the body, and yet it boasts of great things. See how great a forest is set aflame by such a small fire! (v. 5)

A tiny spark holds the power to destroy thousands of acres of forest. Such is the power of the tongue. "Like fire when it is controlled, the tongue held in check is a power for great good. But out of control what havoc both can cause!"[1]

The Tongue: Necessary but Dangerous

In the next three verses, James elaborates on the image used in verse 5.

> And the tongue is a fire, the very world of iniquity; the tongue is set among our members as that which defiles the entire body, and sets on fire the course of our life, and is set on fire by hell. (v. 6)

As usual, James doesn't mince his words or his metaphors! Notice the phrase "the very world of iniquity." James means that

1. Curtis Vaughan, *James: A Study Guide* (Grand Rapids, Mich.: Zondervan Publishing House, 1969), p. 69.

the whole world of evil finds its expression through the tongue. Boastful pride, destructive anger, cutting bitterness, flattering lust—the tongue communicates them all.

Another interesting term in verse 6 is the word for "hell." Instead of using the familiar term *Hades*, James uses *Gehenna*, which was in that day an actual valley outside Jerusalem that was used as a garbage dump. All the filth of the city accumulated there, just as all the evil of our hearts seems to accumulate on our tongues.

In the next two verses, James changes images. Go to any Ringling Bros. and Barnum & Bailey circus and you'll see the truth of what he says.

> For every species of beasts and birds, of reptiles and creatures of the sea, is tamed and has been tamed by the human race. But no one can tame the tongue. (vv. 7–8a)

We know how to train seals, lions, elephants, and others—just think of Gentle Ben, Lassie, Flipper, Shamu. But there's one beast not even P.T. Barnum could tame—the tongue.

With another click of his shutter, James gives us a third and final picture.

> It is a restless evil and full of deadly poison. (v. 8b)

Our tongues are like the forked menace of a poisonous snake. With them we strike and poison those around us. Remember Hitler's words when he bared his fangs against Christianity?

> Nothing will prevent me from tearing up Christianity, root and branch. . . . We are not out against a hundred-and-one different kinds of Christianity, but against Christianity itself. All people who profess creeds . . . are traitors to the people. Even those Christians who really want to serve the people . . . we have to suppress. I myself am a heathen to the core.[2]

This same venomous hatred later resulted in the production of Cyclon B gas, the poison used to kill millions at Auschwitz, Dachau, Treblinka, and elsewhere.

---

2. Adolf Hitler, as quoted by Spiros Zodhiates in *The Behavior of Belief* (Grand Rapids, Mich.: William B. Eerdmans Publishing Co., 1959), p. 115.

The Tongue: Helpful but Inconsistent

The tongue is a powerful, dangerous beast. But remember that we said only *sometimes*. Sometimes it helps mend bones instead of breaking them; sometimes it builds people up instead of tearing them down; sometimes it brings life instead of death. In verses 9–10, James illustrates the tongue's Jekyll-and-Hyde tendency.

> With it we bless our Lord and Father, and with it we curse men, who have been made in the likeness of God; from the same mouth come both blessing and cursing. My brethren, these things ought not to be this way.

But they are. In his book *The Behavior of Belief*, Spiro Zodhiates tells this story.

> A large family sat around the table for breakfast one morning. As the custom was, the father returned thanks, blessing God for the food. Immediately afterward, however, as was his habit, he began to grumble about hard times, the poor quality of the food he was forced to eat, the way it was cooked, and much more. His little daughter interrupted him with, "Father, do you suppose God heard what you said a little while ago?" "Certainly," replied the father with the confident air of an instructor. "And did He hear what you said about the bacon and the coffee?" "Of course," the father replied but not as confidently as before. And then his little girl asked him again, "Then, Father, which did God believe?"[3]

The answer is both, because both reveal the real condition of the heart.

Next, James shows how the human heart is like nothing in nature.

> Does a fountain send out from the same opening both fresh and bitter water? Can a fig tree, my brethren, produce olives, or a vine produce figs? Nor can salt water produce fresh. (vv. 11–12)

3. Zodhiates, *The Behavior of Belief*, pp. 119–120.

Unlike humankind, nature is consistent. Peach trees don't produce poisonous mushrooms. Only the human heart is capable of producing such inconsistencies.

Application

Here are three simple statements concerning the tongue to help you remember the truths James has given us. First, the tongue *defiles*. Remember Jesus' words in Matthew 15—it's actually the heart which is defiled. Second, the tongue *defies*. It defies every attempt at human control. Third, the tongue *displays* what you really are. Justin, one of the early Church fathers, once said,

> By examining the tongue, physicians find out the
> diseases of the body; and philosophers, the diseases
> of the mind and heart.[4]

Open your mouth and stick out your tongue. Now say "Ahhh." Hmmm. Your tongue looks healthy, but what has it revealed about your heart this past week?

Living Insights

James 3:1–12 is replete with rich images that communicate volumes about the tongue. This richness of imagery is paralleled in the book of Proverbs. Let's look at some references there to see what Solomon has to say about the subject. In the space provided, describe what each metaphor means.

A fountain of life (Prov. 10:11) _____

_____

A healing agent (12:18) _____

_____

A tree of life (15:4) _____

_____

---

4. Justin, as quoted in *The International Dictionary of Thoughts*, comp. John P. Bradley, Leo F. Daniels, and Thomas C. Jones (Chicago, Ill.: J.G. Ferguson Publishing Co., 1969), p. 726.

Something more precious than gold and jewels (20:15) _____

_____

What image would people use to describe your conversations?

_____

_____

_____

_____

_____

Which problems relating to the tongue do you struggle with?

Complaining	Talking crudely
Bragging	Talking flippantly
Lying	Talking condescendingly
Gossiping	Talking too much
Criticizing	Talking abrasively

With which one do you struggle most? _____

What can you do to bridle that quality? _____

_____

 Questions for Group Discussion _____

In today's passage we learned that we need to tame our tongues in the same way that a bit directs a horse. If we're to keep our words from trampling others, we must pull back on the reins and bring them under control. When we consider whether or not to say something, we need to weigh whether or not our intended speech is wise.

1. According to the following passages, what characterizes the words of the wise?

Proverbs 11:11	Proverbs 15:7
Proverbs 15:2	Ecclesiastes 10:12

2. Describe an example from your life when your speech was wise.

3. According to the following passages, what characterizes the words of the fool?

   Proverbs 10:14   Proverbs 18:6

   Proverbs 11:11   Proverbs 18:7

   Proverbs 15:2   Ecclesiastes 10:14

4. Describe an incident when your speech was foolish. If you could relive that experience, what would you say (or not say) instead?

5. How will you apply these Scriptures about wise and foolish speech to your life to let your words build up rather than tear down?

6. What does your day-to-day speech reveal about your heart? If others used your words to measure your character, would they see a person of integrity?

Chapter 8

THE WISE, THE UNWISE, AND THE OTHERWISE
(PART ONE)
James 3:13–16

Borrowing on old woodsmen's proverb, Carl Sandburg recapped his biography of Abraham Lincoln with a chapter titled, "A Tree Is Best Measured When It's Down."[1] The chapter carefully measures the tall, stately life of a president who was felled by an assassin's bullet.

This proverb aptly testifies about all our lives: only after a person's death can we begin to measure the impact of their life. This was especially true of a poet-king who prefigured Lincoln—Solomon. A glance at his life reveals an author, poet, songwriter, artist, king, diplomat, theologian, teacher, zoologist, psychologist, philosopher, financier, engineer, and architect.

How could Solomon's success grow to such unparalleled heights? 2 Chronicles 1 holds the answer. Beginning in verse 6,

> Solomon went up there before the Lord to the bronze altar which was at the tent of meeting, and offered a thousand burnt offerings on it. In that night God appeared to Solomon and said to him, "Ask what I shall give you." (vv. 6–7)

Solomon had just begun his reign when God made him this incredible, unconditional offer. To Solomon's credit, he did not respond with greed. Instead, he humbly praised God for His goodness, which then led to his request.

> Solomon said to God, "You have dealt with my father David with great lovingkindness, and have made me king in his place. Now, O Lord God, Your promise to my father David is fulfilled, for You have made me king over a people as numerous as the dust of

1. Carl Sandburg, *Abraham Lincoln: The Prairie Years and The War Years,* one-volume edition (New York, N.Y.: Harcourt Brace Jovanovich, Publishers, 1982), p. 728.

the earth. Give me now wisdom and knowledge, that I may go out and come in before this people; for who can rule this great people of Yours? (vv. 8–10)

Solomon asked for only two things, wisdom and knowledge. Not the theoretical kind of knowledge that could grapple with abstract matters, but the ability to apply divine truth to daily life. Although Solomon was an intelligent, well-educated king, he recognized that he lacked wisdom that only God could provide. His humility of heart greatly pleased God.

> God said to Solomon, "Because you had this in mind, and did not ask for riches, wealth, or honor, or the life of those who hate you, nor have you even asked for long life, but you have asked for yourself wisdom and knowledge that you may rule My people over whom I have made you king, wisdom and knowledge have been granted to you. And I will give you riches and wealth and honor, such as none of the kings who were before you has possessed nor those who will come after you." (vv. 11–12)

A thousand years after Solomon's day, James wrote a letter to a group of Jews who had been driven from their homeland by persecution. He explained that trials are inevitable and that they occur for a purpose (James 1:2–4). For that purpose to be worked out in their lives, one ingredient was essential—*wisdom*. So James counseled his readers to follow Solomon's example and ask for it!

> But if any of you lacks wisdom, let him ask of God, who gives to all generously and without reproach, and it will be given to him. (v. 5)

James mentions the word *wisdom* only one other time in his letter. In chapter three, which deals with the tongue, James begins with a sober warning about becoming teachers, then discusses the two basic tools all teachers use to communicate truth—their tongues (3:1–12) and their lives (vv. 13–18). The remaining verses develop the importance of *wisdom* in the life of a teacher. Not human wisdom, mind you, but divine wisdom. The kind we all need to ask for—as Solomon did.

Tests of True and False Wisdom

As is true of all valuable possessions, wisdom has its counterfeits. So, beginning in verse 13, James teaches us how to recognize the genuine article.

Divine Wisdom: Genuine

Let's look carefully at the two specific tests of someone who is wise.

> Who among you is wise and understanding? Let him show by his good behavior his deeds in the gentleness of wisdom. (v. 13)

The first test James mentions is *good behavior*. The word translated *behavior* has a root idea of changing or returning to the truth. With this phrase, James is saying that a wise person is someone whose life is changing in accordance with the truth of God's Word.

Another test of true wisdom is *gentle deeds*. Today people tend to associate the word *gentleness* with being a jellyfish—something spineless and spiritless. In James's day, however, quite the opposite was true. This word was used to describe bringing a high-spirited horse under control. The spirit and strength of the horse weren't lost; they were simply harnessed. Gentleness also referred to a brilliant teacher who could debate others without getting angry or a soothing medicine that brought comfort to a painful wound.

The qualifications for being wise have nothing to do with your I.Q. or your ability to pack away facts or your impressive eloquence. The test of wisdom is a life that is patterned after truth and is under control.

One of the greatest problems among new Christians is the desire to hit the road with a running start to set the world straight. Typically, the first place their sneakers stop is their home. Upon arrival, they declare spiritual martial law and billy-club family members with Bible verses every time one of them steps out of line. And then these new believers can't understand why their loved ones don't stand in line to enlist in the ranks and sing "Onward Christian Soldiers." What's lacking in these new believers? *Wisdom*—balanced by the gentleness and control that Paul carefully described to his young friend Timothy.

> The Lord's bond-servant must not be quarrelsome, but be kind to all, able to teach, patient when

wronged, with gentleness correcting those who are
in opposition. (2 Tim. 2:24–25)

Wisdom is not just accurate words spoken, but the gentle spirit in
which they are spoken.

Human Wisdom: Counterfeit

In contrast to divine wisdom, which is characterized by a changed
and controlled life, James reveals the marks of human wisdom.

But if you have bitter jealousy and selfish ambition
in your heart . . . (James 3:14a)

Did you notice the phrase "in your heart?" These two marks,
jealousy and selfish ambition, are deeply embedded motives in the
unwise heart. People often confuse jealousy with its evil twin, envy.
What's the difference? Envy begins with empty hands and mourns
for what it does not have. Jealousy begins with full hands but is
threatened by the thought of losing what it possesses. James is saying
that an unwise person is someone who tends to be suspicious,
resistant, and given to rivalry.

The second mark—selfish ambition—is the desire to be seen,
quoted, and respected (see Matt. 23:1–7). It's the motive that drives
people to push themselves to the top. Paul refers to such people in
Philippians 1:15–17, who preached Christ "out of selfish ambition
rather than from pure motives." These men hungered for the prom-
inence of position, not for gentleness and good behavior. The wise,
however, allow God to open doors instead of trying to force them
open themselves.

Characteristics of False Wisdom

In the second half of verse 14, James argues for rooting out
these hidden motives, saying, in effect, "If this is down deep in your
heart, don't keep on as if it weren't! Face it, deal with it as sin,
confess it and seek wisdom." He goes on to heighten the urgency
of his request by revealing five characteristics of false wisdom.

. . . do not be arrogant and so lie against the truth.
This wisdom is not that which comes down from above,
but is earthly, natural, demonic. (James 3:14b–15)

Arrogant

The first of the ugly faces of false wisdom is arrogance—rationalizing your own sins or even boasting that the end justifies the means, that the bad done wasn't all that bad, or that everybody does it. In ancient times, the word was used to describe a person who boasted about winning an election dishonestly.

Unfortunately, many in the church today attempt to shelter their arrogance under the umbrella of grace. But grace doesn't excuse sin, and make no mistake about it, arrogance *is* sin (see 4:16).

Theologian Charles Hodge explained the relationship between divine grace and the human heart.

> The doctrines of grace humble man without degrading him and exalt him without inflating him.[2]

Now that's *true* wisdom.

Lying against the Truth

How do Christians justify their arrogance? By lying against the truth. The natural inclination of human wisdom is not simply to ignore or dodge the truth; it is to lie against it. The *New English Bible* renders this phrase, "a defiance of the truth."

When a life is out of step with Scripture, there will eventually be a manipulation of the truth to justify following a drumbeat different from God's. The result is self-deception. It's like getting the first wall up on a new home and suddenly realizing that your measurements are wrong. But instead of admitting the mistake, you design a new ruler to fit the inaccurate measurements of the first wall. The entire house ends up a crooked disaster.

Earthly

According to verse 15, false wisdom has an earthly origin. It views everything from a strictly horizontal perspective: earthly success, earthly standards, earthly motives, earthly attitudes, earthly methods, earthly everything!

---

2. Charles Hodge, as quoted by Spiros Zodhiates in *The Behavior of Belief* (Grand Rapids, Mich.: William B. Eerdmans Publishing Co., 1959), p. 142.

Natural

An adequate rendering of the word *natural* is *soulish*, meaning "fleshly, not related to the Spirit of God." It denotes a wisdom whose vision is limited to things temporal, not eternal.

Demonic

This mindset is characteristic of demons. They are brilliant and know a great deal—even about God—but there is no change, no obedience, and no yielding of self to God.

Results of False Wisdom

In verse 16, James reminds us first of the roots of false wisdom—bitter jealousy and selfish ambition—then he identifies the fruit.

> For where jealousy and selfish ambition exist, there is disorder and every evil thing. (v. 16)

Disorder

By *disorder*, James means more than just confusion. He means disharmony, antagonism, and the absence of unity and stability. When a teaching results in rivalry, rather than building up in love, it is not wisdom from above.

Every Evil Thing

When human wisdom is taught, it lifts the lid on all sorts of worthless, petty, evil things. Like Pandora's box, the human heart is home to a haunting array of sinful thoughts (Mark 7:20–23).

Conclusion

While it's true that a tree is best measured when it's down, the fruit of a tree is best measured when it's up. In Matthew 12:33, Jesus said that a tree is known by its fruit. What are the fruits of your life? Do people see good behavior and gentleness or disorder and every evil thing?

By the end of Solomon's life, the royal tree that once stood so straight and tall had rotted from within. Although in the springtime of his life he had written, "The fear of the Lord is the beginning of knowledge; / Fools despise wisdom and instruction" (Prov. 1:7), by the autumn of his life he had ceased fearing God and depended on his own human wisdom. Once the world's wisest man—now the world's wisest fool.

Living Insights

God told Solomon he could ask for anything he wanted. Sounds like a child's dream—to rub a magic lamp and get a genie who grants three wishes, doesn't it? But God is not a genie. He does, however, grant wishes to His children. But He does so purposefully, not arbitrarily. Let's examine this thought further by turning again to Solomon.

Read 2 Chronicles 1:1–12. How did Solomon respond to God's question?

_____

_____

Why did God reward Solomon with riches, wealth, and honor as well as knowledge and wisdom?

_____

_____

If Solomon, who was granted both knowledge and wisdom by God, could grow to be a fool, how can we make sure that we stay wise?

_____

_____

When God grants us wisdom, how can we guard against letting our divine wisdom make us proud or arrogant?

_____

_____

_____

James 1:5 promises that God gives wisdom generously to all who ask Him. In what matters do you need God's wisdom today?

_____

_____

_____

Write your request for wisdom to Him on the following lines. When you need His wisdom again, remember that He promises to give it to us generously. Ask Him for it.

_____

_____

_____

_____

 ## Questions for Group Discussion

After reading a passage like James 3:13–16, the question for each of us to think over is, "Am I living wisely?" Let's try to uncover some possible answers through the following questions.

1. Do you ever struggle with jealousy? If so, what do you think drives your emotional desire to be jealous?

2. Reviewing what you learned in today's lesson, how is envy different from jealousy?

3. If the tendrils of selfish ambition have taken root in your life, describe any poisonous fruit this plant has produced.

4. Jealousy and selfish ambition do not exist in some display case in a musty museum; they are on display in our own lives. Think about a situation where these twin destroyers wreaked their havoc through you. What led up to it, and how do you think you might have prevented it?

5. How can God's wisdom help you realign your perspective and behavior with His?

6. What is the connection between your prayer life and the wisdom you possess?

Chapter 9

THE WISE, THE UNWISE, AND THE OTHERWISE
(PART TWO)
James 3:13, 17–18

Few places are more barren or more desolate than the Libyan Desert. Bounded on the north by the Mediterranean Sea, the east by Egypt, the south by Chad, and the west by Algeria, this scorched plain of sand and rocky plateaus is home to but a few wandering nomads.

That's what makes it so incredible that an emerald Eden could thrive in the heart of this North African desert. But one did. Miles of green, luxuriant crops and ripening fruit swayed against the backdrop of an endless, sand-colored emptiness.

For such a garden to grow in the naturally parched soil, a commodity very unnatural to the desert had to be piped in—water! Through an experiment designed to test whether a desert could be a productive place, water was pumped from distant wells into vast reservoirs. Then seeds were planted, and the transformation that followed was nothing short of a miracle. The experiment proved that, if sufficient water was provided, the desert could produce.

Why are we starting a message on James 3 in the middle of the Libyan Desert? Because it graphically illustrates what James teaches. Without the Savior, our lives are like that parched, unproductive desert. A desolation exists in our souls that ruins rather than rejuvenates. Listen as James describes the desert condition of our natural wisdom.

> But if you have bitter jealousy and selfish ambition in your heart, do not be arrogant and so lie against the truth. This wisdom is not that which comes down from above, but is earthly, natural, demonic. For where jealousy and selfish ambition exist, there is disorder and every evil thing. (James 3:14–16)

For divine wisdom to take root in our lives, something very unnatural to our hearts must be piped in by faith—the living water of the Savior (John 7:38). Under the Holy Spirit's supervision, our lives can blossom with a divine wisdom we could never produce on our own.

Tests of True Wisdom

In our last lesson, we learned that the tests of true wisdom are good behavior and gentleness (James 3:13). In a word, good behavior means *change*—an inner willingness to obey God's Word. Gentleness refers to *strength under control,* like that seen in a high-spirited horse that has been well trained.

Characteristics of Divine Wisdom

When these two divinely encoded seeds—good behavior and gentleness—are sown, they produce a totally unnatural, even supernatural crop. You won't find any of it at your local grocery store, but you can see at least seven harvests of divine wisdom on display in our passage today.

> But the wisdom from above is first pure, then peaceable, gentle, reasonable, full of mercy and good fruits, unwavering, without hypocrisy. (James 3:17)

Let's take some time to inspect each of these harvests.

Purity

"But the wisdom from above is *first* pure." The word *first* not only means first in a list, but also first in importance. The primary harvest of divine wisdom is purity. The word means "freedom from defilement, without contamination, clean." It suggests not only moral cleanliness, but also purity of motive—the same kind Peter refers to in his admonition to wives of unbelieving husbands.

> In the same way, you wives, be submissive to your own husbands so that even if any of them are disobedient to the word, they may be won without a word by the behavior of their wives, as they observe your chaste and respectful behavior. (1 Pet. 3:1–2)

Peter instructs these wives to bring their husbands back to Christ through good behavior with pure motives. The term for *chaste* refers to the same inner purity of motive that James addresses.

Purity also carries with it a peculiar promise. Jesus said, "Blessed are the pure in heart, for they shall see God" (Matt. 5:8). But the

69

Bible also teaches that no man has seen God (John 1:18). Then what did Jesus mean? He meant that the pure in heart will know God so intimately that they will see Him come to their rescue when tempted or come alongside as their closest friend when facing trials. Purity clears our vision to see Him at work in everything we do.

Peace

Notice the difference between the divine harvest of peace and the natural products of human wisdom, which are listed in verse 14: bitter jealousy, selfish ambition, arrogance, and lying. Clearly, we are prone by nature to quarrel. But when wisdom from above fills our hearts, a peaceable nature blossoms, one that helps heal relationships rather than tear them apart.

Now, some may say, "Well, I'm not by nature a calm and peaceable person." That's the whole point. None of us are peaceable by nature. Remember, we are like the desert. But when God's wisdom rains gently upon that desert, a peaceable attitude springs to life.

Gentleness

The Greek term for *gentle* in verse 17, *epieikes*, is different from the term James used four verses earlier. This new term is hard to explain, because it means more than any one English word can convey. Some have rendered it "equitable, fair, or moderate." "Tolerant" would be better, but even it falls short. Perhaps William Barclay captured the meaning best when he said,

> The man who is *epieikes* is the man who knows when it is actually wrong to apply the strict letter of the law. He knows how to forgive when strict justice gives him a perfect right to condemn. He knows how to make allowances, when not to stand upon his rights, how to temper justice with mercy, always remembers that there are greater things in the world than rules and regulations. . . . Matthew Arnold called it "sweet reasonableness" and it is the ability to extend to others the kindly consideration we would wish to receive ourselves.[1]

1. William Barclay, *The Letters of James and Peter*, rev. ed., The Daily Bible series (Philadelphia, Pa.: Westminster Press, 1976), pp. 95–96.

Reasonableness

As you might suspect form Matthew Arnold's description of what *gentle* means, there's a close connection between it and the next characteristic, being *reasonable*. Like two corresponding pieces of a puzzle, gentleness and reasonableness fit snugly together because of their subtle differences. The word *gentle* is really written for those in places of authority over others. *Reasonable*, on the other hand, is especially fitting for those who are under someone else's authority.

The original term comes from two Greek words that combine to mean "easily persuaded." It's the opposite of being stubborn and obstinate. This quality is reflected by those who are open, conciliatory, and easy to work with.

A classic example of someone who acted reasonably is recorded in Genesis 13. It's the story of how Abraham (still called Abram at this point in his life) settled a prosperity problem that arose with his nephew Lot.

> Now Abram was very rich in livestock, in silver and in gold. . . . Lot, who went with Abram, also had flocks and herds and tents. And the land could not sustain them while dwelling together, for their possessions were so great that they were not able to remain together. (vv. 2, 5–6)

Notice how Abraham, the older of the two, took the initiative to create a compromise.

> So Abram said to Lot, "Please let there be no strife between you and me, nor between my herdsmen and your herdsmen, for we are brothers. Is not the whole land before you? Please separate from me; if to the left, then I will go to the right; or if to the right, then I will go to the left." (vv. 8–9)

Now that's reasonable! Are you that kind of person? Can you give serious thought to an opinion that differs from yours without feeling threatened or getting angry?

Full of Mercy and Good Fruits

The natural wisdom we inherit from our flesh infuses us with cynicism and harshness, especially toward the sufferings of others. The wisdom that comes down from above, however, reacts to suffering with mercy and good fruits. Mercy is a compassionate *attitude*, and good fruits are *actions* that naturally flow from mercy.

In the first century, the word *mercy* was commonly used to describe people's feelings toward someone who had suffered unjustly. In the New Testament, however, this same word is used several times to describe the attitude a believer should have toward those who suffer due to problems they have caused themselves.

Surprised? Anyone can feel for people who suffer through no fault of their own, but God's mercy enables us to have pity and compassion for those who have caused their own sorrow. This divine mercy then issues forth into practical help: "good fruits." William Barclay wrote, "We can never say that we have truly pitied anyone until we have helped him."[2]

Unwavering

The original term for *unwavering* means "a person of fixed principles." Unwavering believers faithfully adhere to the principles in God's Word regardless of the circumstances. Though others may say, "When in Rome, do as the Romans do," this individual lives under the precept, "When in Rome, do as the believer should do."

Coupled with an unwavering fidelity to truth, this individual is decisive, one who is not afraid to make decisions based on Scripture.

Without Hypocrisy

Our modern word *hypocrisy* comes from the first-century term *hupokrites*, used to describe actors. In Greek theater, actors normally played several parts by simply wearing a different mask for each character. Today when we use the word *hypocrite* we mean anyone who wears masks—who pretends to be someone he or she is not.

True wisdom is never two-faced or deceptive. It is completely and simply honest.

The Result of True Wisdom

Now that we've looked at the harvests, let's step back and see what result divine wisdom can have in our lives.

> And the seed whose fruit is righteousness is sown in
> peace by those who make peace. (James 3:18)

2. Barclay, *Letters of James and Peter*, p. 97.

James at a Glance

Main Theme: Real faith produces genuine works.

Key Section: 2:14–20, "Faith, if it has no works, is dead . . ."

Key Terms: *Faith, Works, Doers, Brethren*

FAITH	WORKS		CHAPTER SECTIONS
When **STRETCHED,** faith doesn't break;	it produces genuine **STABILITY.**	C H A P T E R 1	1. Greeting (v. 1) 2. Trials of Life (vv. 2–12) 3. Temptations to Sin (vv. 13–18) 4. Response to Scripture (vv. 19–27)
When **PRESSED,** faith doesn't fail;	it produces genuine **LOVE.**	C H A P T E R 2	1. Partiality and Prejudice (vv. 1–13) 2. Indifference and Intellectualism (vv. 14–20) 3. Obedience and Action (vv. 21–26)
When **EXPRESSED,** faith doesn't explode;	it produces genuine **CONTROL** and **HUMILITY.**	C H A P T E R S 3,4	1. Expressions of Words—The Tongue (3:1–12) 2. Expressions of Attitudes—The Heart (3:13–4:12) 3. Expressions of Desires—The Will (4:13–17)
When **DISTRESSED,** faith doesn't panic;	it produces genuine **PATIENCE.**	C H A P T E R 5	1. Money Matters (vv. 1–12) 2. Sickness and Sin (vv. 13–18) 3. Carnality and Correction (vv. 19–20)

The ABCs of James

Author: James, the half brother of Jesus. See Matthew 13:55, John 7:5, 1 Corinthians 15:7, Galatians 1:19.

Background: The difficult circumstances of the scattered saints of that day caused many to drift spiritually. This led to unwise and unbridled speech, wrong attitudes toward God and fellow Christians, strife, gross carnality, and unproductive faith.

Characteristics: James has been called "the Proverbs of the New Testament." The book contains many practical, straightforward exhortations and great emphasis upon the importance of balancing right belief with right behavior. It includes many Old Testament references and word pictures.

Destination: Christians "dispersed abroad" in the first century. (James 1:1).

Era: Between A.D. 45 and 50. James is the earliest of the New Testament books.

To understand this verse, you must remember that, in James, peace means being rightly related to one another. It's not a vertical peace between God and man; it's a horizontal peace between human beings. Those who disturb this peace between themselves and others will not enjoy a righteous lifestyle before God. Those who maintain peaceful relationships without violating God's standards are producing the fruit of righteousness.

Nothing is more barren and desolate than the Libyan Desert—except the human heart apart from God. But as rain can give life to the desert, so God can cultivate a garden of divine wisdom in us through the living water of His Holy Spirit. Are you ready to shift from being a harvest watcher to a harvest producer? Take a moment now to begin watering the seeds of His wisdom with this prayer from Saint Francis of Assisi.

> Lord, make me an instrument of Your peace!
> Where there is hatred, let me sow love;
> Where there is injury, pardon;
> Where there is doubt, faith;
> Where there is despair, hope;
> Where there is darkness, light;
> Where there is sadness, joy.
> O Divine Master, grant that I may not so
>   much seek
> To be consoled, as to console;
> To be understood, as to understand;
> To be loved as to love.
> For it is in giving that we receive;
> It is in pardoning that we are pardoned;
> It is in dying that we are born to eternal life.[3]

---

3. Saint Francis of Assisi, as quoted by Spiros Zodhiates in *The Behavior of Belief* (Grand Rapids, Mich.: William B. Eerdmans Publishing Co., 1959), pp. 181–82.

 *Living Insights*

Continuing our study of James 3:17–18, we want to hold these verses up to the light again to be sure we catch every facet of this dazzling jewel called divine wisdom.

Wisdom is reasonable and easily persuaded. If you are under someone's authority, whether in the family or at work, are you cooperative or resistant to their leadership?

_____

_____

_____

In what way have you come to terms with the place of authority and how to work wisely under those who lead you?

_____

_____

_____

How do 1 Peter 2:13–17 and Romans 13:1–7 contribute to your thinking on this?

_____

_____

_____

Wisdom is full of mercy and good fruits. If your eyes are sensitized, you cannot help but see incredible suffering around you. Mercy is exercised when compassion for an individual so grips you that you reach out to offer help. Read James 2:15–16 and Matthew 5:7. Meditate on these verses. Now, name several good fruits that come to mind from some act of mercy you have performed.

_____

_____

_____

Wisdom is unwavering, dependable, and consistent (James 1:6). Joshua and Caleb exhibited such wisdom. Read Numbers 13:17–33 and 14:1–45. Now compare 14:24 with Joshua 14:1–14. What outstanding trait did Caleb and Joshua exhibit?

_____

_____

_____

Wisdom is not hypocritical; it does not put on a false face. Two-faced living reveals a shallow walk. What does Romans 12:9 have to say about two-faced living?

_____

_____

_____

 Questions for Group Discussion

1. According to James 3:17–18, how does human wisdom differ from godly wisdom?

2. How can you tell if you are relying on your own soulish wisdom or on the wisdom that comes from God?

3. If our wisdom flows from impure motives, it is not from God. Have you ever acted to serve yourself and attributed your ideas or actions to spiritual motives? If so, how can you keep this from happening in the future?

4. According to James 3:17, wisdom is peaceable. What is the difference between exhibiting wise peace and exercising peace at all costs? Does being peaceable imply that a wise man or woman never confronts problems?

5. James describes wisdom as unwavering. Another word we could use is constant. When you make decisions, do you base them on constant truths rather than changing circumstances?

6. Are there aspects of your life that others would see as two-faced? If so, how can you remove this hypocrisy from your life?

Chapter 10

HOW FIGHTS ARE STARTED AND STOPPED

James 4:1–10

D id you ever have to eat grass when you were growing up? In my neighborhood, that was the standard punishment for anyone who lost a fight. Victor and spectators jeered and howled while the vanquished grazed. Then we would all go play again . . . until the next fight. Fighting, playing, eating a little Saint Augustine, that's just how it was—and how it still is. Oh, we may not eat grass anymore or play as much, but we still love to fight.

Franklin Roosevelt once said, "There is nothing I love as much as a good fight."[1] Fighting is something that comes to us naturally. Why? Because we're each born with a scrappy nature that prefers going for the jugular to giving in.

The fact that we have a pugnacious nature is not a new problem, either. Beginning in a field with Cain and Abel, human history is more easily traced by the bloody path of its fights than by its accomplishments. That path, sad to say, also cuts right through the church. Denominations bomb one another in Ireland, seminaries clash over doctrines, authors attack other authors in print, and on it goes, right down to the squabbles of individual saints.

It isn't surprising, then, that James addresses the problem of conflicts among Christians. Fighting, worshiping, fighting some more—it was the same two thousand years ago as it is today.

Let's listen as James jumps into the fray with some hard-hitting advice about how fights are started and stopped.

Initial Facts

The break between chapters 3 and 4 is an unfortunate one, since James neither changes the subject nor shifts his emphasis. In fact, his comments regarding the destructive nature of the tongue, which started in chapter 3, build to a crescendo in the fourth

---

1. Franklin D. Roosevelt, as quoted in *Bartlett's Familiar Quotations*, 15th ed., rev. and enl., ed. Emily Morison Beck (Boston, Mass.: Little, Brown and Co., 1980), p. 779.

chapter, beginning with the rhetorical question,

> What is the source of quarrels and conflicts among
> you? (4:1a)

Before we look at James's answer to this question, let's establish
who "among you" refers to. If you'll look back to 3:1 and ahead to
4:11, you'll see that everything between these two verses is directed
toward Christians.

Notice also how James describes the fighting by using two words
that form one unit. In Greek, *quarrels* is the general term for an
entire war, and *conflicts* refers more to individual battles.

Like a parent stepping into the middle of a sibling squabble, James
asks his readers, "What started all this?" But before any finger pointing can start, James points his finger at the first of two root causes.

Analysis of the Problem

To expose the first root cause, James answers his first rhetorical
question with a second.

First Cause: Inner Desire

> Is not the source your pleasures that wage war in
> your members? (4:1b)

The Greek term for *pleasures* means "desire or passion." It's a
neutral term that, depending on the context, can refer either to
evil or good desires. When our desires go unmet, however, our
frustration mounts and eventually erupts into conflict. So we wage
war, intent on fighting until we get our way.

Next, James mentions three specific effects of this unchecked,
combative desire.

> You lust and do not have; so you commit murder.
> You are envious and cannot obtain; so you fight and
> quarrel. You do not have because you do not ask.
> (v. 2)

Certainly most of us are not guilty of murder in a literal sense,
but we do kill with our thoughts. We allow ourselves to calculate
ways to assassinate someone else's character. "But at least it doesn't
go any further than that," some may rationalize. Oh, yes it does.
Those same murderous thoughts spur us on to the second effect
James mentions: fights and quarrels—wounding with words.

The third effect is failure to pray. Why? Because we're too busy fighting. We prefer to slug things out rather than surrender the situation to God.

James not only analyzes the problem of fighting, he also anticipates a fighter's response. Such is the case in verse 3. The apostle envisioned people protesting, "But we did ask God, and He didn't answer our prayers," to which James replies,

> You ask and do not receive, because you ask with wrong motives, so that you may spend it on your pleasures.

Commentator Curtis Vaughan explains,

> Their requests were legitimate, but the reason for making them was illegitimate. They wanted only to satisfy their own cravings, pamper their own passions. God's glory, God's service, consideration for other people—none of these things entered into their thinking. Such prayers are an insult to God.[2]

Prayer—real prayer—allows God to come to our rescue His way.

Second Cause: "Kosmos" Motivation

Another cause for quarrels among believers is found in verse 4.

> You adulteresses, do you not know that friendship with the world is hostility toward God? Therefore whoever wishes to be a friend of the world makes himself an enemy of God.

In the New Testament, the Greek term for "world," *kosmos*, is ordinarily used to mean "the world apart from God." It signifies a self-centered, Satan-controlled philosophy that is hostile toward God. Believers war when they attempt to satisfy their inner desires by worldly motivation. *Kosmos motivation* means handling conflicts by fighting, pushing, and demanding until you get exactly what you want, when you want it. It's saying, "Lord, Your way is not the best way for me. I know what's best, and I will satisfy my needs by doing it the world's way instead of Yours."

---

2. Curtis Vaughan, *James: A Study Guide* (Grand Rapids, Mich.: Zondervan Publishing House, 1969), p. 85.

What does kosmos motivation result in? First, it creates hostility toward God. Deliberately living according to the world's standards rather than God's is an act of rebellion. The second effect James mentions is enmity against God. Commentator Donald W. Burdick writes,

> To have a warm, familiar attitude toward this evil world is to be on good terms with God's enemy. It is to adopt the world's set of values and want what the world wants instead of choosing according to divine standards. The person who deliberately "chooses . . . to be a friend of the world" by that choice "becomes an enemy of God."[3]

Let's pause for a moment and consider some specific examples of what James is talking about. If you are a person gifted with leadership capabilities that are not being used, you may have a tendency to be impatient and manipulate circumstances to push yourself to the front. God says, "Wait, let Me open the doors I want you to walk through. Take advantage of this time away from the limelight to deepen your trust in Me."

If you are single and eager to be married, you may be tempted to panic and hurry into a marriage relationship. But God's advice would be, "Don't run ahead of Me; I know your desires. Lean on Me and I'll help you find the right future."

Or perhaps you've worked hard and done a good job, but somebody else received the credit. The world says that you should fight for your rights! Promote yourself, because if you don't, then nobody else will. But God instructs, "There's no need to clamor for recognition. You're here to do your work for My glory, not yours. I have seen the good that you have done and I will reward you."

See how easily our inner desires can become frustrated and how quickly our life's goal can shift from pleasing God to fighting for ourselves?

Synopsis of the Solution

Having diagnosed the causes and effects of our fighting, James next turns our attention to God's solution.

---

3. Donald W. Burdick, "James," in *The Expositors Bible Commentary* (Grand Rapids, Mich.: Zondervan Publishing House, Regency Reference Library, 1981), vol. 12, p. 193.

The Power

> Or do you think that the Scripture speaks to no
> purpose: "He jealously desires the Spirit which He
> has made to dwell in us"? (v. 5)

The first part of the solution is the power of the Holy Spirit.
God has given us His Spirit because He jealously desires, as one
commentator put it, "the entire devotion of the heart."[4]

> God claims us entirely for Himself. No alien rela-
> tionship, such as friendship with the world, will be
> tolerated by Him. He wants the undivided devotion
> of every human heart.[5]

When believers divide their allegiance between the Lord and
the world, they end up fighting. But when we draw upon the power
of His Holy Spirit and say, "Lord, it's Your battle, please take control," the fighting subsides.

The Principle

The second part of God's solution is found in verse 6:

> But He gives a greater grace. Therefore it says, "God
> is opposed to the proud, but gives grace to the humble."

Greater grace is the principle. God is saying, "I'll give abundant
grace to those who are willing to humble themselves and wait. Trust
Me and draw your strength from Me."

Practical Advice

James closes with some seasoned practical advice. Notice how
he uses the word humble to bracket verses 7–9. In verse 6 we're
told that God gives greater grace to the humble, and in verse 10
we're reminded again to humble ourselves. What comes between
is a series of commands that describes the process of becoming
humble in God's sight.

> Submit therefore to God. Resist the devil and he
> will flee from you. Draw near to God and He will

---

4. J. B. Mayor, as quoted by Vaughan in *James: A Study Guide*, p. 88.

5. Vaughan, *James: A Study Guide*, p. 88.

draw near to you. Cleanse your hands, you sinners;
and purify your hearts, you double-minded. (vv. 7–8)

First, *submit to God.* We are to cease fighting and surrender our wills to His control. Second, *resist the devil.* We are to resist the prompting of the god of this world that tells us to assert ourselves, which often leads to conflict. Third, *draw near to God.* We are to stay close to God by developing a loving companionship. Fourth, *cleanse hands and purify hearts.* We are to cleanse ourselves from any moral defilement that may have created enmity between ourselves and others or God.

In verse 9, we see James's earnestness as he appeals for godly sorrow, the intense kind that grows out of a deep awareness of our sin.

Be miserable and mourn and weep; let your laughter
be turned into mourning, and your joy to gloom.

Finally, James sums up his advice on how fights are stopped.

Humble yourselves in the presence of the Lord, and
He will exalt you. (v. 10)

Humble yourselves. Say "uncle" to the Spirit's prompting and surrender to God, letting Him do your fighting.

If you live your life fighting, you'll end up on the ground and, over a lifetime, you'll end up eating a lot of grass. Wouldn't you prefer surrendering to the One who promises to lift you up? Which will it be: a mouthful of grass or a life full of grace?

Living Insights

Humility is the mother of all virtue. Every good quality in a person's life is conceived within the womb of that one quality. Read through the following Scriptures and jot down what they have to say about humility.

Job 5:11 _____

Psalm 138:6 _____

Proverbs 15:33 _____

Proverbs 16:19 _____

Micah 6:8 _____

81

Matthew 18:4 _____

Luke 14:11 _____

One impediment to becoming a humble person is the "pride of life" (1 John 2:16), which comes from an unhealthy love for the world. In a terse, prescriptive manner, James 4:7–10 gives us the steps to breaking off our adulterous love affair with the world. Many of the commands in these verses have consequences attached to them. List the commands in the first column, and if they have results, list those in the second.

James 4:7–10

Command	Result
1. _____	_____
2. _____	_____
3. _____	_____
4. _____	_____
5. _____	_____
6. _____	_____
7. _____	_____
8. _____	_____
9. _____	_____
10. _____	_____

How was the principle in James 4:10 illustrated by Jesus' life (see Phil. 2:5–11)?

_____

_____

_____

How could it be illustrated in your life (see Phil. 2:3–4)?

_____

_____

_____

Questions for Group Discussion

1. According to James 4:1, what is the general source of our conflicts?

2. From verses 2–3, what are some of the specific causes and effects of conflict?

3. What traits from verses 2–3 cause most of your conflicts?

4. How are you affected when you give in to these traits?

5. What can you do to take that problem by the root and pull it out of your life?

Chapter 11
THE PERIL OF PLAYING GOD
James 4:11–17

Years ago Eric Berne wrote a best-seller titled *Games People Play.* In it he exposed the subtle ways people manipulate others without their awareness of what's happening. Three years later a parallel book, *Games Christians Play,* took readers behind the scenes in the Christian community to reveal the games played beneath a religious veneer.

For example, have you ever encountered the "When you have been a Christian as long as I have . . ." game player? These people were either born in a choir loft or saved at age two. Their favorite ploy? Putting others down by "subtly" displaying their own superior knowledge or experience.

To illustrate, let's say you're an excited new Christian, and you share with one of these smug pillars of the faith that you discovered the book of Habakkuk. You can expect the typical put-you-in-your-place response: "Oh, so you're just now getting into Habakkuk? Well, you'll just love it when you discover the Chaldean taunt-songs in chapter 2. Why, I remember studying that years ago when I was a missionary living with a migrant family. Of course, when you've been a Christian as long as I have . . ."

Another game believers love to play is: "I'd love to, but . . ." Imagine that your pastor asks you to help lead vacation Bible school. What do you do? If you hesitate, you're a goner. So you say,

> "Oh, I'd love to, but I have seven small children under four . . ." Or: "My pet ocelot died and we're holding a memorial service . . ." Or: "My invalid aunt lives with me, and she's afraid of the dark . . ." But after this happens once or twice, whenever your name is mentioned, someone will automatically mumble, "Can't . . . dead ocelot . . . afraid of the dark," and pass on to the next name.[1]

---

1. Judi Culbertson and Patti Bard, *Games Christians Play* (New York, N.Y.: Harper and Row Publishers, Harrow Books, 1967), pp. 8–9.

Now you may think these games and others like them are unique to this century, but they're not! Games were afoot among first-century believers as well. In fact, in our passage today, James introduces us to the most widely played game among Christians then and now: playing God.

It's not too difficult to figure out why we're so eager to play this game. Since the day Satan subtly manipulated Adam and Eve into playing his rebellion game, all of us have been born with a natural passion for wanting to be God in our own lives and the lives of others.

This aggressive desire to assert ourselves is what causes Christians to fight, as James noted earlier. He explained that, when it comes to having our desires met, we basically have two choices: we can either fight to satisfy them ourselves, or we can humbly allow God to fulfill them by surrendering to His control. James urged humility, but he knew that there were many who would choose instead to play God.

Listen carefully as James reveals the objectives and rules of this perilous game and provides a crucial evaluation of it.

When "Playing God" with Others

To begin, James addresses those whose favorite pastime is playing God with others.

The Objective

> Do not speak against one another, brethren. He who speaks against a brother or judges his brother, speaks against the law and judges the law; but if you judge the law, you are not a doer of the law but a judge of it. (James 4:11)

Written between the lines of this verse is the objective of the game: imagine yourself as superior to other Christians, and put them down in various ways.

The Rules

Also found in verse 11 are the rules for playing God with others. Rule one: If you want to play God with others, you need to speak against your brother or sister. The Greek term translated *speak against* comes from a combination of two words meaning *to talk down*. It's the idea of talking about one person to another with the goal of lowering your listener's estimate of that third person.

Of course, those who play this game do so only when the persons being talked about are not around to defend themselves. And there is usually little concern about accuracy. All of this is neatly covered up, however, with phony words such as, "Stop me if I'm wrong, but . . ." or "Perhaps I shouldn't say this, but . . ." or "I don't mean to be critical, but . . ."

The second rule is that you must judge others. The word *judge* in verse 11 means "to pronounce condemnation upon someone." To judge someone rightly, however, we must know *all* there is to know about that other person. It requires the kind of complete understanding about a person's thoughts and motives that only God possesses.

Jesus condemns a judgmental attitude in his illustration about the splinter and the plank.

> "Do not judge so that you will not be judged. For in the way you judge, you will be judged; and by your standard of measure, it will be measured to you. Why do you look at the speck that is in your brother's eye, but do not notice the log that is in your own eye? Or how can you say to your brother, 'Let me take the speck out of your eye,' and behold, the log is in your own eye? You hypocrite, first take the log out of your own eye, and then you will see clearly to take the speck out of your brother's eye." (Matt. 7:1–5)[2]

Another reason for not judging is that when we criticize others, we speak against the law and judge it. The law James is probably referring to in chapter 4, verse 11, is the royal law he quoted in his second chapter, "You shall love your neighbor as yourself" (2:8). Commentator Curtis Vaughan explains,

> The meaning is this: The man who deliberately breaks the law thereby disparages that law. In effect he sets himself above it and declares that it is a bad law, not worthy to be obeyed. Such a person removes himself from the category of a *doer* of the law and becomes a *judge* of the law.[3]

---

2. Jesus and James are not saying that discernment isn't necessary. They are only condemning the kind of critical attitude that seeks to condemn. For further study, read 1 Kings 3:9–12; Galatians 6:1; Hebrews 5:14; and James 5:19–20.

3. Curtis Vaughan, *James: A Study Guide* (Grand Rapids, Mich.: Zondervan Publishing House, 1969), pp. 93–94.

The Evaluation

James now evaluates the game and states the reasons why it has no place in the believer's life.

> There is only one Lawgiver and Judge, the One who is able to save and to destroy. (4:12a)

The first reason believers should avoid playing this game is that it places us in a position of authority reserved for God alone. Only God has the ability to save and destroy, which proves that only He is qualified to judge. Second, playing God ignores or excuses our own failures.

> But who are you who judge your neighbor? (v. 12b)

In the Greek, the personal pronoun *you* is placed first in the sentence—"You there! Who are you . . . ?"—turning the spotlight away from others and putting its full force on ourselves. Commentator Donald W. Burdick writes:

> With shattering bluntness, James crushes any right his readers may have claimed to sit in judgment over their neighbors. This is not to rule out civil courts and judges. Instead, it is to root out the harsh, unkind, critical spirit that continually finds fault with others.[4]

When "Playing God" with Yourself

Perhaps the most self-deluding of all games is that version of playing God that we play out in our own lives.

The Objective

The objective for this version of playing God is written between the lines of verses 13–17. It says: Imagine yourself as the final authority over your life, then live like it. Take God completely out of the picture; don't depend on Him; don't even recognize His existence.

The Rules

Now let's examine the rules, which are revealed in verse 13.

> Come now, you who say, "Today or tomorrow

---

4. Donald W. Burdick, "James," in *The Expositor's Bible Commentary* (Grand Rapids, Mich.: Zondervan Publishing House, Regency Reference Library, 1981), vol. 12, p. 196.

we will go to such and such a city, and spend a year there and engage in business and make a profit."

Let's break this passage down and study the five rules we can infer from what James describes. Rule one: Selfishly choose your own time and schedule ("Come now, you who say, 'Today or tomorrow'"). Rule two: Select the location that pleases you ("we shall go to such and such a city"). Rule three: Limit your stay to please yourself ("and spend a year there"). Rule four: Arrange your activities so that they work primarily for your own benefit and pleasure ("and engage in business"). Rule five: Predict your success and boast about it ("and make a profit").

James is not criticizing planning or advocating haphazard organization. We know from Scriptures such as Proverbs 21:5 that God encourages wise planning. But our plans are always to be made according to His will, acknowledging His sovereignty over our lives.

Then what is James attacking? The kind of horizontal thinking that presumptuously plans as though God did not even exist.

The Evaluation

Beginning in verse 14, James lays down several reasons why we can never win at playing God in our own lives.

> Yet you do not know what your life will be like tomorrow. (4:14a)

Tomorrow's circumstances are totally uncertain. An unexpected injury, the sudden death of a spouse, the loss of a job—these or a host of other surprises can instantly and completely change our lives.

Another reason is that we have no assurance of a long life.

> What, after all, is your life? It is like a puff of smoke visible for a little while and then dissolving into thin air. (v. 14b PHILLIPS)

Moses expressed this same truth in Psalm 90:

> You speak, and man turns back to dust. A thousand years are but as yesterday to you! They are like a single hour! We glide along the tides of time as swiftly as a racing river, and vanish as quickly as a dream. We are like grass that is green in the morning but mowed down and withered before the evening shadows fall. (vv. 3–6 LB)

The third reason is that we have no right to ignore God's will.

> Instead, you ought to say, "If the Lord wills, we will
> live and also do this or that." (James 4:15)

It is the height of arrogance to disregard God as the master of our fate. As Psalm 14:1 says, "The *fool* has said in his heart, 'There is no God'" (emphasis added). It's a fool's game to play God; nevertheless, James knows that some would rather take the risk and play than humbly submit to the Lord.

> But as it is, you boast in your arrogance; all such
> boasting is evil. (James 4:16)

Evil. All the reasons against playing this game are summed up in this one word.

When You Want to Stop "Playing God"

Quitting this game won't be easy; but for those who want out, James leaves two simple rules to follow.

> Therefore, to one who knows the right thing to do
> and does not do it, to him it is sin. (v. 17)

First, *you must know the right thing to do.* You must stop and evaluate your life, whatever the cost, in light of the truth of God's Word.

Second, *you must start doing the right thing.* Take what you learn from studying God's Word and begin practicing it. Stop running others down and let God do the judging. Instead of seeking to control, learn to submit to God and follow.

Are you willing to stop playing God and humbly submit instead? What are you saying in your heart right this moment? "Yes" or "Well, you know I'd really love to, but my pet ocelot just died and . . ."

Living Insights

One way to play God is to imagine yourself as your own final authority—who doesn't need to give any recognition to God. The underlying assumption is that you become the controller of your destiny.

Reread James 4:14–16 to see how James counters this perilous game. As you fill in the blanks below from 4:14, really stop and remember Who is in control.

> "Yet you do not know what your life will be like _____. You are just a _____ that appears for a little while and then _____."

How will these words cause you to look to your Creator rather than to your own resources?

_____

_____

_____

Look again at verse 15. Who determines your tomorrows? How does that change the way you look at your future plans?

_____

_____

_____

While you may plan to carry out your daily responsibilities, your attitude should reflect submission to God. What does James say in verse 16 about giving yourself the credit?

_____

_____

_____

Are you playing a game in which the stakes are higher than you anticipated? Playing God is perilous. It hurts others and removes you from God's will. Take a few moments to name the first move you are going to make to remedy this dilemma.

_____

_____

_____

_____

Questions for Group Discussion

1. Have you ever spoken against a brother or a sister in a judg-mental way? How did he or she receive it?

2. What is the difference between being judgmental and using good judgment?

3. When is it appropriate to approach a brother or sister with your concerns about his or her life?

4. When is it *in*appropriate to approach him or her?

5. Have you ever been accused of being judgmental when you were approaching a brother or sister with godly motives? How did you respond?

6. If you have unconfessed sin in your own life, how can you deal with it so that you won't be hypocritical when approaching another person about his or her sin?

7. Assuming that you don't have a "log in your eye," should you always approach a brother or sister when you see sin in their lives? Why or why not?

Chapter 12

WARNINGS TO THE WEALTHY
James 5:1–6

In 1923 the world's most successful financiers met at the Edgewater Beach Hotel in Chicago. Those present included the president of the largest independent steel company, the greatest wheat speculator, the president of the New York Stock Exchange, a member of the President's Cabinet, the greatest bear on Wall Street, the president of the Bank of International Settlement, and the head of the world's greatest monopoly. According to one source,

> Collectively, these tycoons controlled more wealth than there was in the United States Treasury, and for years newspapers and magazines had been printing their success stories and urging the youth of the nation to follow their examples.[1]

Two decades later a follow-up study was conducted to discover the rest of the story about these seven men who met in Chicago. The results were stunning. The steel magnate lived in debt his last five years and died penniless. The wheat speculator died insolvent overseas. The president of the New York Stock Exchange had been released from New York's Sing Sing state prison. The Cabinet member received a pardon from prison to die at home. The Wall Street bear, the president of the Bank of International Settlement, the head of the monopoly—all committed suicide.[2]

All seven success stories ended tragically. Names that were once synonymous with wealth, power, and influence were, in the end, associated with humiliation, crime, and violent death. It may take intelligence to make a lot of money, but it takes true wisdom to handle it.

In our lesson today, it's probable that James had in mind the same kind of wealthy and influential individuals as those men who met at Edgewater Beach Hotel. He begins chapter 5 with the sharp address, "Come now, you rich . . ."—which J. B. Phillips translates, "And now, you plutocrats . . ."

1. Paul Lee Tan, *Encyclopedia of 7,700 Illustrations* (Rockville, Md.: Assurance Publishers, 1979), p. 824.

2. Tan, *Encyclopedia of 7,700 Illustrations*, p. 824.

In James's day, Rome was a *plutocracy*—a government by the wealthy. They controlled the legal system like their own chess set and often caused Christians to be persecuted. Like the individuals in James 4:13 who *planned* as if there were no God, this oppressive class *spent* as though there were no God.

Introductory Clarifications

Before we begin our lesson, we need to emphasize that it is *not* true that the poor go to heaven and the rich go to hell. As simpleminded as this idea sounds, it is nevertheless a belief common to many. However, eternal life and earthly possessions are not that easily sorted out. In fact, there are at least four general classifications of people and possessions that we can identify.

First, *those who are poor without and poor within*. "Poor without" means they possess little of this world's goods. The millions who struggle for survival every day would be in this group. "Poor within" means that they are unbelievers, people who have not accepted God's priceless gift of His Son as their Savior.

Second, *those who are rich without and rich within*. These are individuals, like Joseph or Job, who are rich economically and spiritually.

Third, *those who are poor without and rich within*. These individuals have little in the way of possessions, but are born again. Most of us would consider ourselves in this category. We must be careful, however, that we aren't measuring what poor means by the standard of our neighbor's possessions. Are we saying we're poor because we barely have the necessities of food and shelter, or are we saying that we're poor because we have only two cars and the person next door has three and a boat?

Fourth, *those who are rich without and poor within*. This is the group James addresses—the *unbelieving* plutocrats.

Expository Instruction

Following a general rebuke in verse 1, James gives several specific statements that can be divided into two lines of thought. First, the reasons for the rebuke and, second, promises of divine judgment. Let's start with the rebuke.

General Rebuke

Come now, you rich, weep and howl for your miseries which are coming upon you. (James 5:1)

93

With his usual frankness, James unflinchingly confronts wealthy unbelievers with their doom. He says, "Weep and howl," which, in Greek, suggests more than just a little boo-hooing; it means shrieking and loud lamentations.

Why should the rich, who have limitless power and every comfort at the tips of their bejeweled fingers, shriek and writhe in misery? James graphically reveals the reasons in his next few verses.

Human Reasons

James's first reason was that the rich were guilty of hoarding their wealth.

> Your riches have rotted and your garments have become moth-eaten. Your gold and your silver have rusted. (vv. 2–3a)

In those days, a person could display wealth basically three ways: food, clothing, and precious metals—the coin of the land. Those who were wealthy ate well, dressed extravagantly, and spent lavishly. James also introduces the three basic ways that time and disuse rob a person's hoarded wealth: food rots, clothes become moth-eaten, and gold and silver tarnish. And just as riches spoil, so does the spirit of those who hoard. Time and disuse turn people's attitudes toward life into bitterness and disappointment.

The second reason the rich faced doom was because they cheated others.

> Behold, the pay of the laborers who mowed your fields, and which has been withheld by you, cries out against you; and the outcry of those who did the harvesting has reached the ears of the Lord of Sabaoth. (v. 4)

William Barclay conveys the seriousness of this crime in his illumination of this passage.

> The day labourer in Palestine lived on the very verge of starvation. His wage was small; it was impossible for him to save anything; and if the wage was withheld from him, even for a day, he and his family simply could not eat. That is why the merciful laws of Scripture again and again insist on the prompt payment of his wages to the hired labourer. "You

shall not oppress a hired servant who is poor and needy. . . . You shall give him his hire on the day he earns it, before the sun goes down (for he is poor, and sets his heart upon it); lest he cry against you to the Lord, and it be sin in you" (Deuteronomy 24:14,15). . . . "Woe to him that builds his house by unrighteousness and his upper rooms by injustice; who makes his neighbor serve him for nothing, and does not give him his wages" (Jeremiah 22:13). "Those that oppress the hireling in his wages" are under the judgment of God (Malachi 3:5). . . .

Here it is said that the cries of the harvesters have reached the ears of the Lord of hosts! . . . It is the teaching of the Bible in its every part that the Lord of the universe is concerned for the rights of the labouring man.[3]

Third, James rebuked the rich for living a totally selfish lifestyle.

You have lived luxuriously on the earth and led a life of wanton pleasure; you have fattened your hearts in a day of slaughter. (v. 5)

The picture James depicts here is a vivid one of unrestrained self-gratification. "Eat, drink, and be merry. Get fat," and James adds, "get slaughtered."

In his commentary on James, Spiros Zodhiates writes,

When the author was in Rome, one of the most interesting places he visited was the Palace of Nero. . . . Apparently Nero and his friends liked to eat and fare sumptuously. In the middle of the main dining room was something that looked like a well. When asked what it was used for, the guide replied that Nero and his guests used to eat so much that they could not hold it any more, so they had to vomit the food they just ate, and this was the place where they did it. Then back they went to the

3. William Barclay, *The Letters of James and Peter*, rev. ed., The Daily Study Bible Series (Philadelphia, Pa.: Westminster Press, 1976), pp. 118–119.

tables. . . . Such was the life of the notorious Nero. He was a man, but he lived like a pig.[4]

Those who raise livestock say that to get a pig ready for slaughter, you simply pen it up and keep shoveling in the food. Every day the pig adds more and more weight, eating itself right into the slaughterhouse. "Why should I shriek?" Nero might have sneered. And the Bible faithfully answers, "Because you have satiated your stomach and your heart with this world's pleasures and starved the poor man whose work has provided your wealth, all the while ignoring the judgment that awaits this wanton self-indulgence."

The last reason for James's rebuke is that the rich were taking advantage of the righteous.

> You have condemned and put to death the righteous
> man; he does not resist you. (v. 6)

James has already accused the rich of dragging believers into court (2:6). Now he charges them with murder. Some teach that the righteous man refers to the Lord Jesus or the first martyr, Stephen. But the wording seems broad enough to include all the righteous who had been victimized by wealthy unbelievers.

Divine Retribution

Woven into the fabric of our passage are four promises of judgment. Let's go back to verse 1 and pick up the threads of divine retribution.

First: *Hoarded riches reap miserable dividends* (vv. 1–3a). The dividends are bitterness, cynicism, disappointment, and emptiness, to name a few. Study the selfishly wealthy, and you'll see the miserable face of Charles Dickens's Ebeneezer Scrooge.

Second: *Riches provide no relief in eternity* (vv. 3b and 5b). Solomon, one of the richest men who ever lived, wrote:

> Riches do not profit in the day of wrath,
> But righteousness delivers from death. (Prov. 11:4)

After we die, God will never ask to look at the balance in our bank account. The only balance that will matter then is whether the righteousness of Christ has been credited to our account through

---

4. Spiros Zodhiates, *The Behavior of Belief* (Grand Rapids, Mich.: William B. Eerdmans Publishing Co., 1959), p. 67.

faith in Him. Those whose accounts show only a negative balance of sin will have to pay the penalty of eternity in hell (John 3:36).

Third: *The unjust acts of the unsaved are not forgotten* (James 5:4b). One of the most serious scenes in all Scripture depicts the unsaved appearing before the Great White Throne to be judged (Rev. 20:11–15). Even though, for a little while, it may appear as if the unbelieving wealthy do not have to answer to anyone for their selfish ways, the day is coming when they will shriek in anguish as they are judged according to their deeds, which are written in God's Book.

Fourth: *James implies throughout his message that a lack of judgment today does not mean a lack of judgment tomorrow.* Jesus pictured this promise of divine judgment in the parable of the rich man and Lazarus. The rich man was poor within; he lived in luxury while Lazarus, covered with sores, begged for crumbs from his table. When death came for both, an angel took Lazarus to the "bosom of Abraham," meaning heaven, while the rich man, in Hades, "lifted up his eyes, being in torment" (Luke 16:23). Judgment had come, and it was final. Why? Because he was rich? No. Because he was an unbeliever while on earth. He glutted himself with perishable items while ignoring his impoverished, imperishable soul.

Applicatory Lessons

To reinforce our understanding of James's teaching, let's turn to another biblical writer, Paul, for a couple of practical lessons.

Lesson one: *God's concern is not with actual wealth, but with our attitude toward wealth.*

> If we have food and covering, with these we shall be content. But those who want to get rich fall into temptation and a snare and many foolish and harmful desires which plunge men into ruin and destruction. For the love of money is a root of all sorts of evil, and some by longing for it have wandered away from the faith, and pierced themselves with many griefs. (1 Tim. 6:8–10)

Did you notice the two contrasting attitudes? God wants us to have an attitude of contentment (v. 8), not a constant craving for riches. The Lord is not condemning the rich, but He is judging those who long to be rich.

97

Lesson two: *God's counsel is not against people who are wealthy, but against the wrong priorities of the wealthy.*

> Instruct those who are rich in this present world not to be conceited or to fix their hope on the uncertainty of riches, but on God, who richly supplies us with all things to enjoy. Instruct them to do good, to be rich in good works, to be generous and ready to share, storing up for themselves the treasure of a good foundation for the future, so that they may take hold of that which is life indeed. (vv. 17–19)

Being wealthy has its own peculiar risks and pressures that twist priorities. Two that Paul mentions are becoming conceited and trusting in wealth for security. The proper priorities are fixing our hope on the Lord and being rich in good works.

Concluding Thought

Has there ever been a time in your life when you became rich within? Ephesians 1:7 says,

> In [Christ] we have redemption through His blood, the forgiveness of our trespasses, according to the riches of His grace.

For just a moment, forget about your bank account and consider your soul's account. Do you possess the riches of His grace through faith in Christ?

Living Insights

Each of us fits into one of four categories of wealth listed at the beginning of our study. Some have few material goods and are bankrupt within. Others have both material and inward riches. There are some who are not affluent but are inwardly wealthy. And finally, many have abundant outward wealth but their souls are impoverished.

As we saw in our lesson, it was this last category that captured James's interest. He used four characteristics to describe these people: hoarding, cheating, living selfishly, and taking advantage of the godly. It's important to note that wealth itself is not denounced in Scripture. It is the love of money that is labeled evil (1 Tim. 6:10).

What is your attitude about money?

_____

_____

_____

In his book *Master Your Money*, Ron Blue, a financial consultant, offers the four following guidelines to help you assess your relation to material wealth.[5] They are: God owns it all; we are in a growth process; the amount is not important; and faith requires action.

According to Matthew 25:14, God has entrusted His possessions to us. We are merely His stewards. How does this truth affect the way you spend His money that He has entrusted to you?

_____

_____

_____

As the owner of everything, God has all the rights. As the steward, you have responsibilities and rewards. Name a few responsibilities and rewards you have as a manager of God's resources.

_____

_____

_____

_____

Look at Matthew 25:21. If we are faithful with what He entrusts to us, what happens?

_____

_____

_____

5. Ron Blue, *Master Your Money* (Nashville, Tenn.: Thomas Nelson Publishers, 1986), pp. 19–23.

Are there ways you could be more faithful with what He has entrusted to you? If so, what are they?

_____

_____

_____

_____

What is your strategy for being more faithful with what the Lord gives you?

_____

_____

_____

_____

Questions for Group Discussion

1. What little things have you been faithful with in the past that resulted in God entrusting you with more responsibility?

2. In what current little thing is your faithfulness being tested?

3. How are you doing in this area of stewardship?

4. When you are not faithful in the little things, what should you do?

5. Does your concern for your physical wealth sometimes overshadow your interest in your spiritual wealth?

6. If God knocked on your door today, would he be pleased with your stewardship of His resources? Why or why not?

Chapter 13

DOING RIGHT WHEN YOU'VE BEEN DONE WRONG

James 5:7–12

W alk away," says that small but definite voice inside you.

"Wait a minute!" says a louder voice. "That guy in the parking space next to mine just banged my car with his door!"

"Just walk away," says the persistent small voice.

"Sure, I nicked his car with my door, but it didn't even leave a mark. This guy just put one of those quarter-sized dents in mine!"

"Just walk away," says the small voice, which, in spite of its size is nonetheless getting annoying.

"I think I'll go put a couple of quarter-sized dents in this guy's head!" says the big voice, sounding very mean.

"C'mon now, just walk away."

Our Natural Reaction

Walking away sounds cowardly, doesn't it? Our nature prompts us to fight back. "Revenge is a kind of wild justice,"[1] said Francis Bacon. And Lord Byron claimed, "Sweet is revenge."[2] Fighting back helps us get where we want to go; it helps us protect our interests and defend our territory.

But God hates retaliation games. He sees them take place between husbands and wives, parents and children, brothers and sisters. He hates the sneaky uppercuts between boss and employee. And He especially despises the clawing He tearfully observes in the church. Oh, how He wishes we would learn how to respond rightly when we have been done wrong.

1. Francis Bacon, as quoted in *The Harper Religious and Inspirational Quotation Companion*, comp. and ed. Margaret Pepper (Great Britain: André Deutsch, 1989; New York, N.Y.: Harper and Row, Publishers), p. 361.

2. Lord Byron, as quoted in *Bartlett's Familiar Quotations*, 15th ed., rev. and enl., ed. Emily Morison Beck (Boston, Mass.: Little, Brown and Co., 1980), p. 460.

God's Supernatural Alternative

God wants us to overcome our natural reaction with a supernatural response. We'll discover this response in Peter's first letter, then we'll see how to apply it in the fifth chapter of James's letter. Let's look first at Peter's counsel.

> Servants, be submissive to your masters with all respect, not only to those who are good and gentle, but also to those who are unreasonable. For this finds favor, if for the sake of conscience toward God a person bears up under sorrows when suffering unjustly. For what credit is there if, when you sin and are harshly treated, you endure it with patience? But if when you do what is right and suffer for it you patiently endure it, this finds favor with God. (1 Pet. 2:18–20)

Enduring "good and gentle" treatment is a piece of cake. And enduring suffering that comes as a result of sin is nothing extraordinary. However, enduring *unfair* treatment with patience is a novelty.

When we respond in such a supernatural way, God is pleased. Peter says twice in this passage that "this finds favor" with God (vv. 19, 20). The word for *favor* in the original Greek text is *charis* —"grace." God considers patient endurance of injustice a grace, something commendable because it is beyond ordinary human response.[3]

Now that we know what God expects, let's turn to James 5 to discover God's four-point plan for making this supernatural response a part of our daily experience.

Exposition of the Passage

James is placing a large package before us. When we start to open it, we'll find another package within the larger one. As we keep opening, another package and yet another will be revealed, much like a toddler's stacking cups, one inside the next. As God develops one quality in our lives toward the goal of doing right when we've been wronged, we will find that there is yet another quality to unwrap. Keep unwrapping until you have opened all four. Don't give up after opening only the first one!

---

3. See Edwin A. Blum, "1 Peter," in *The Expositor's Bible Commentary* (Grand Rapids, Mich.: Zondervan Publishing House, Regency Reference Library, 1981), vol. 12, pp. 234–235.

General Observations

Before we tear into these packages, let's make some observations about James 5:7–12 that will give us some perspective.

First, *the passage is addressed to the believer*. The word *brethren* is mentioned four times in this passage (vv. 7, 9, 10, 12). The kind of patient endurance to which James is referring is found only in a person whose daily life is connected to God. This is not something unbelievers can muster up themselves. God must be "mustering" it in us.

Second, *these six verses are directly related to the previous six*. As we saw in our last lesson, rich tyrants were oppressing the righteous, their treacherous acts extending all the way to murder (v. 6). Just as he finishes exposing their crimes, James turns a corner (v. 7) and begins giving the Christian victims advice on how to live in this intolerable situation.

Third, *James's advice is found in four commands—two positive and two negative*. The first two are given in a tense that essentially says, "Do this right now." The last two, being negative, are saying, "Don't even start that habit" or "Stop doing this!"

Fourth, *woven into these verses are four vivid illustrations that shed light on each command*. Perhaps more than any other writer of Scripture, James is a vivid illustrator. He opens the shades on the windows of our understanding to let the light pierce through, giving us no reason to miss his meaning.

Now let's look at the specifics of what he says.

Specific Explanation

Be patient. Upon opening the first package, we find that God wants us to cultivate patience.

> Therefore be patient, brethren, until the coming of the Lord. (v. 7a)

In Greek, *patient* is actually a combination of two words: *makros*, meaning "a long way, far," and *thumos*, meaning "passion, heat, rage, or anger." Hence, we have the concept of "long-suffering" or taking a long time to get angry. To put it in simplest terms, patient people are not short-tempered, but have a long fuse.

Two things are particularly impressive about this quality. First, it is love's first response. Remember the very first definition of love from 1 Corinthians 13? "Love is patient" (v. 4)—it "suffereth long," as the King James Version puts it. Love will motivate a person to overlook the offense, to delay the anger, to suffer long. Second, patience is essential to learning. There's an ancient Greek motto that goes something like this: "The first necessity of learning is patience." When we're irritable and impatient, we can never learn the lessons God has for us.

Now let's see how James illustrates this quality.

> The farmer waits for the precious produce of the soil, being patient about it, until it gets the early and late rains. You too be patient. (vv. 7b–8a)

Some of the richest farmland in the world is found in parts of Palestine, but most of the time—as a result of external oppression—the Jews were consigned to farming in the hill country where there was no irrigation and the soil was difficult to till. It was back-breaking work for Mr. Jewish Farmer, whose rock-tossing chores seemed never to end.

When the soil was finally prepared and the seed sown, his eyes gazed heavenward for signs of rain. After all the hard work, would the whole endeavor be for naught because of no rain? The early rains of October and November would break the stifling heat of summer and help the seed to germinate. The winter months would then bring a period of dormancy. And the latter rains, which would come in the springtime months of April and May, would allow the plants to mature. So, in order for the farmer to receive a good crop, he would have to wait. A premature planting or untimely harvest could spell disaster.

You just can't hurry God's plan.

That's why James mentions the Lord's return in verse 7a. He is speaking not only of the Second Coming, but also of how the Lord comes to our rescue in times when we've been wronged. We are to be patient, just as the farmer patiently waits for God to bring rain.

Strengthen your heart. Now that we've opened James's first package, let's untie the ribbon on the second.

> Strengthen your hearts, for the coming of the Lord is near. (v. 8b)

Isn't James insightful? He knows that people who refuse to fight often retreat into their own self-pity instead of into the arms of God.

Therefore, this package is labeled "strengthen your heart."[4] The idea is "to prop up or support something that's heavy." When you've been done wrong, your heart is heavy. So James says to let the Lord support your heart and help you in this situation (see Ps. 55:22; 1 Pet. 5:7).

One way to utilize this package is through the 50:20 principle. Taken from Genesis 50:20, this principle will help you strengthen your heart by changing your focus. Let's take a brief look at the story of Joseph to uncover the specifics of this principle.

If you remember his story, you will recall the roller-coaster life Joseph had. His father's favorite son, he was also his brothers' favorite punching bag. After they sold him as a slave, he worked hard at earning his master's respect. However, he was falsely accused by the boss's wife and unjustly thrown in prison. While there, he saved a man's life, but the man quickly forgot him. Finally remembered, he interpreted Pharaoh's troubling dream and was promoted to second-in-command over all Egypt. When he eventually met his brothers again, he pronounced these words:

> "As for you, you meant evil against me, but God
> meant it for good . . ." (Gen. 50:20)

Rather than looking at ourselves or the unfair circumstances, the 50:20 principle enables us to focus on God. When we apply this guideline, we are freed up to see God as our teacher and the other person as a tool for making us into the people He intended us to be.[5]

Do not complain. So far we've opened two packages, one labeled "be patient" and the other labeled "strengthen your heart." Now let's take the paper off the third.

> Do not complain, brethren, against one another, so
> that you yourselves may not be judged; behold, the
> Judge is standing right at the door. (James 5:9)

The word translated *complain* literally means "to groan or sigh." This groaning reveals an internal, unexpressed attitude of bearing

---

4. The phrase "strengthen your hearts," as rendered in the NASB, is the literal translation. However, the NIV helps us understand the sense of the phrase better by saying that we are to "stand firm" in the faith and not doubt that God will vindicate the righteous.

5. For another example of this principle in action, see David's response to Shimei in 2 Samuel 16.

a grudge, which is the forerunner to deep-seated bitterness and hatred. It also merits the judgment of God, who "is standing right at the door." To help us resist this grudging spirit, James uses two illustrations—first directing our attention to the Old Testament prophets and then to Job.

> As an example, brethren, of suffering and patience, take the prophets who spoke in the name of the Lord. We count those blessed who endured. (James 5:10–11a)

We need to read only a few verses of Hebrews 11 to get an idea of what the prophets had to face and how they endured. While some of them "conquered kingdoms, performed acts of righteousness," and "obtained promises" (v. 33), others "were tortured . . . experienced mockings and scourgings, yes, also chains and imprisonment. They were stoned, they were sawn in two, they were tempted, they were put to death with the sword" (vv. 35b–37a). But like Stephen in Acts 7, these suffering saints did not dishonor God by casting blame or bearing grudges; they exemplified endurance in the midst of terrible trials. As did Job.

> You have heard of the endurance of Job and have seen the outcome of the Lord's dealings, that the Lord is full of compassion and is merciful. (James 5:11b)

William Barclay deepens our understanding of Job's endurance.

> We generally speak of the *patience* of Job which is the word the Authorized [King James] Version uses. But patience is far too passive a word. . . . As we read the tremendous drama of his life we see him passionately resenting what has come upon him, passionately questioning the conventional arguments of his so-called friends, passionately agonizing over the terrible thought that God might have forsaken him. . . . But the great fact about him is that in spite of all the agonizing questionings which tore at his heart, he never lost his faith in God. . . . "I know that my redeemer lives" (Job 19:25). His is no unquestioning submission; he struggled and questioned, and sometimes even defied, but the flame of his faith was never extinguished.

The word used of him is that great New Testament word *hupomonē*, which describes, not a passive
patience, but that gallant spirit which can breast the
tides of doubt and sorrow and disaster and come out
with faith still stronger on the other side. . . . It
was the faith which held grimly on that came out
on the other side, for "the Lord blessed the latter
days of Job more than his beginnings" (Job 42:12).[6]

Now we come to our last package of the four, titled *do not swear.*

But above all, my brethren, do not swear, either
by heaven or by earth or with any other oath; but
your yes is to be yes, and your no, no, so that you
may not fall under judgment. (v. 12)

The Greek word for *swear*, as used in the New Testament, means
"to grasp something sacred firmly, for the purpose of supporting
what you're saying or doing." Christians shouldn't have to rely on
this, because our words should be so riveted to truth that swearing
or using oaths is unnecessary.

Also, in the midst of suffering, it is easy to make oaths we can't
keep. This is because we're caught up in the heat of the moment,
eyes focused only on the present. Instead, we should wait quietly
for the outcome, because that is when insight will come (see v. 11,
"outcome").

Finally, James seems to be advocating plainness of speech for
Christians. Rather than piously invoking a sacred presence upon
all that we say, we should avoid appearing super-spiritual and endure
trials with humility and simplicity.

Wrapping It Up

Walking away when wronged is not a stroll in the park. It's
tough—so tough that it requires supernatural empowering. That's
why these four characteristics are gifts. God wishes to give you these
traits so they can be a comfortable part of your attitudinal wardrobe.
Try one on for size today!

---

6. William Barclay, *The Letters of James and Peter*, rev. ed., The Daily Study Bible series
(Philadelphia, Pa.: Westminster Press, 1976), p. 125.

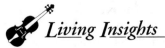

Living Insights

Being misunderstood is one of the hardest grievances to bear. You know you did the right thing. God knows you did the right thing. Unfortunately, no one informed everybody else! Jesus said being harshly treated by the world is par for the course (John 15:18–19).

Let's take a moment to examine two passages of Scripture in which two godly men, Jeremiah and Daniel, suffered unjustly. Read Jeremiah 26:1–16 and Daniel 6:4–28.

What was Jeremiah's righteous behavior? Daniel's?

_____

_____

_____

_____

What did Jeremiah's enemies do? Daniel's?

_____

_____

_____

_____

How did Jeremiah respond to the injustice? Daniel?

_____

_____

_____

_____

Which of James's four directives (*be patient, strengthen your heart, do not complain, do not swear*) do you see illustrated in Jeremiah's life? Daniel's?

_____

_____

On the lines below, write a short prayer to God about the traits that you want Him to deepen in you when you face unjust suffering.

 Questions for Group Discussion

Choosing to do right when we are wronged is one of the hardest decisions to make. When everything within our beings wants vindication, God sometimes calls us to silence.

1. Have you ever had to walk away when someone wronged you? If so, how did walking away require patience?

2. The next time you are wronged unjustly, how will you strengthen your heart? How will you bolster your spirit with God's Word? God's people?

3. Are you still holding a grudge against someone who has wronged you? If so, how can you release your bitterness against that person so it doesn't burn into hatred?

4. Are your words so honest that you never need to swear to convince someone that you're telling the truth? If not, how can you change your words?

5. If we as Christians fail to be true to our words, what does that say to non-Christians about the God we follow?

6. Have you ever thanked God for allowing you to suffer unjustly because He's allowing you to identify with Christ's unjust suffering?

Chapter 14

SUFFERING, SICKNESS, SIN— AND HEALING
James 5:13–16

Splash! Joni Eareckson dove into the Chesapeake Bay a strong, athletic young girl. A split second later she was paralyzed from the neck down, completely helpless, and still under water. Though rescued from drowning by her sister, the doctors could not rescue Joni from the paralysis that swept over her body.

Medically, Joni came to accept the fact that she couldn't be healed. But what about God? Didn't Christ heal all kinds of paralysis and sickness? The more Joni thought and prayed about these things, the more she became convinced God would heal her too. So,

> She brought together a group of friends and church leaders and set up a private healing service. The week before that service, she publicly confessed her faith by telling people, "Watch for me standing on your doorstep soon; I'm going to be healed." On the scheduled day the group read Scriptures, anointed her with oil and prayed in fervent faith. Today, fifteen years later, she is still a quadriplegic. . . . [She] did everything right and seemed to have met all the conditions, yet she was not healed.[1]

Was Joni denied this miracle because she didn't have enough faith? Some believe so. Others say she wasn't healed because of unconfessed sin in her life. Still others would quibble with her about the healing technique she used, saying that healing would come if she followed their three-step process.

What do *you* think?

Today thousands travel around the world seeking those who claim to have the gift of healing. Testimonies of people declaring they have been healed abound. Special "anointed" cloths are even sold that are said to have healing powers. Are these things real?

1. Bruce Barron, *The Health and Wealth Gospel* (Downers Grove, Ill.: InterVarsity Press, 1987), p. 126.

What about the use of medicine? Should we trust God alone for healing? What method does God honor?

What do you think? More important, what does God think? What process does God use to bring about healing? The answers are found in James.

Foundational Facts to Remember

Before we turn to James, however, let's take a brief look at five foundational truths undergirding our current study.

First, *there are two classifications of sin: original and personal.* Original sin refers to the sin nature we inherited from Adam (Rom. 5:12). Personal sin is the daily disobedience that is spawned by our Adamic nature (Rom. 7:14–23). Original sin is the root; personal sin is the fruit.

Second, *original sin introduced sickness and death to the human race.* Romans 5:12 states:

> Therefore, just as through one man sin entered into the world, and death through sin, and so death spread to all men, because all sinned.

Had Adam and Eve never sinned, they would never have died. But because they disobeyed God, sickness and death spread to everyone thereafter. So, in the broadest sense, all sickness and death are the result of original sin.

Third, *sometimes there is a direct relationship between personal sin and sickness.*

Remember the story of David and Bathsheba in 2 Samuel 11 and 12? David committed adultery with Bathsheba, arranged for her husband to be killed, then refused to acknowledge his sin for some time. Finally, after a rebuke from the prophet Nathan, David confessed and repented. Psalm 32 is David's journal of this period. It reveals the physical sufferings he experienced while refusing to acknowledge his sin.

> When I kept silent about my sin, my body wasted away
> Through my groaning all day long.
> For day and night Your hand was heavy upon me;
> My vitality was drained away as with the fever heat of summer. (vv. 3–4)

111

Fourth, *sometimes there is no relationship between personal sin and sickness.* Once when the disciples and Jesus passed by a blind man, they asked,

> "Rabbi, who sinned, this man or his parents, that he would be born blind?" Jesus answered, "It was neither that this man sinned, nor his parents; but it was so that the works of God might be displayed in him." (John 9:2–3)

Fifth, *it is not God's will that everyone be healed.* Paul had the gift of healing (see Acts 20:7–12; 28:7–9), yet he left Trophimus sick in Miletus (2 Tim. 4:20). Epaphroditus almost died while ministering to Paul (Phil. 2:25–27). Timothy, Paul's spiritual son, had a stomach problem and "frequent ailments" (1 Tim. 5:23). Paul asked God three times to remove his own "thorn in the flesh," but God said, "My grace is sufficient for you" (2 Cor. 12:9)—in other words, "No."

Typically, those who claim that is it God's will for everyone to be healed base their belief upon the last phrase of Isaiah 53:5, "And by His scourging we are healed." However, the context of this verse refers to spiritual illness and healing, not physical. Peter underscored this when he wrote,

> And He Himself bore our sins in His body on the cross, so that we might die to sin and live to righteousness; for by His wounds you were healed. (1 Pet. 2:24)

Scriptural Steps to Employ

With these five facts to build upon, let's listen now to James's prescription for those who are suffering, cheerful or sick.

When We Are Suffering

> Is anyone among you suffering? Then he must pray. (James 5:13a)

The Greek term for *suffering* here is literally "in distress." It's a broad term that can mean mental illness, anxiety, or some affliction from which there is no immediate relief. James tells the person, "Pray!" He doesn't promise that if we pray we will be healed; rather, it's as if James is exhorting us to pray for endurance—like Jesus' prayer in John 17:

"I do not ask You to take them out of the world, but to keep them from the evil one." (v. 15)

As we learned from the lives of Paul, Trophimus, Epaphroditus, and Timothy, God sometimes chooses not to remove certain afflictions. Instead, He uses them as tools to strengthen and build us up according to His will.

When We Are Cheerful

Next, James jumps to the opposite extreme—from those who are suffering to those who are cheerful.

Is anyone cheerful? He is to sing praises. (James 5:13b)

Don't feel guilty because you're not experiencing the hardships of others. As Solomon wrote, there is "a time to weep, and a time to laugh; a time to mourn, and a time to dance" (Eccles. 3:4). If you're joyful, James says, let it out! Sing praises and thank God for the blessings He has given.

When We Are Sick

Beginning in verse 14, James introduces the problem of physical illness.

Is anyone among you sick? Then he must call for the elders of the church and they are to pray over him, anointing him with oil in the name of the Lord.[2]

The Greek term used for *sick* means "without strength." It is the idea of being totally incapacitated. What does James recommend in this situation?

First, the one who is sick should take the initiative and summon the elders of the church. There's no way anyone can know you're sick unless you tell them. And yet, many *expect* everyone to somehow know, and then complain when nobody comes to help. When we become seriously ill, our first step is to make others aware of our needs.

2. Some people believe that verse 14 teaches that the clergy, namely priests, are to go to the dying and administer last rights using oil and a special liturgy. However, this passage concerns healing and not dying; restoring to health, not passing away. Others take the view that this verse applied only to the apostles of the first-century church. But James addressed elders, not apostles or "healers"; therefore, it still applies.

Second, the elders are to carry out two functions: anoint and pray (v. 14).

According to the Greek construction of the sentence, the verse actually states, "Let them pray over him, *having* anointed him with oil in the name of the Lord." The anointing should precede the praying.

Typically, the word *anoint* is associated with a religious ceremony where oil is applied to the head (see 1 Sam. 10:1). But, as Jay Adams points out in his book *Competent to Counsel,*

> James did not write about ceremonial anointing at all. . . . The ordinary word for a ceremonial anointing was *chrio* (a cognate of *christos* [Christ] the "anointed One"). The word James used (*aleipho*), in contrast to the word *chrio* ("to anoint"), usually means "to rub" or simply "apply." The word *aleipho* was used to describe the personal application of salves, lotions, and perfumes, which usually had an oil base. . . . It was even used to speak of plastering walls. . . . An *aleiptes* was a "trainer" who rubbed down athletes in a gymnastic school. *Aleipho* was used frequently in medical treatises. And so it turns out that what James required by the use of oil was the use of the best medical means of the day. James simply said to rub oil . . . on the body, and pray. . . . In this passage he urged the treating of sickness by medical means accompanied by prayer. The two are to be used together; neither to the exclusion of the other. So instead of teaching faith healing apart from the use of medicine, the passage teaches the opposite.[3]

Fortunately, our medical expertise has improved from oil to antibiotics, X rays, and laser surgery. And just as the elders in James's days were to see that proper medical treatment was applied, the same is true of elders today.

Third, James recommends that the sick leave the results in God's hands. The elders were to anoint and pray over the sick "in the name of the Lord" (v. 14b), invoking God's will for the situation. That prayer of faith lead to three specific results, found in verse 15.

3. Jay Adams, *Competent to Counsel* (Phillipsburg, N.J.: Presbyterian and Reformed Publishing Co., 1970), pp. 107–108. Compare Mark 16:1 and John 12:3, regarding ceremonial anointing, with Luke 10:33b–34a, which refers to medical anointing.

> And the prayer offered in faith will restore the one
> who is sick, and the Lord will raise him up, and if
> he has committed sins, they will be forgiven him.

The three specific results James mentions are restoration, raising up, and forgiveness. Yes, he addresses the sins of the sick person too. The context clearly indicates that this is a person who is suffering physically as a direct result of personal sin. Evidence for this is found in the Greek word for restoration, *sozo*, meaning "saved." It's the same word James uses in verse 20:

> Let him know that he who turns a sinner from the
> error of his way will save his soul from death and
> will cover a multitude of sins.

"Saving his soul from death" is a reference to restoring someone's fellowship with God. When James says in verse 15 that the prayer offered in faith will *restore* the one who is sick, he means restoring that individual's spiritual life.

The next result is that the Lord will raise the individual up (James 5:15), which refers to physical healing. If a person is physically ill due to unconfessed sin, then by confessing that sin, he or she can be healed physically.[4]

The final result of confessing is God's gracious forgiveness.

Practical Principles to Claim

In summary, let's glean four practical measures to follow—two from verse 16 and two from our passage as a whole.

> Therefore, confess your sins to one another, and pray
> for one another so that you may be healed. The
> effective prayer of a righteous man can accomplish
> much. (v. 16)

First, *confession of sin is healthy—employ it!* Don't let sins build up in your life to the point that they make you physically ill. William Barclay writes,

> In a very real sense it is easier to confess sins to
> God than it is to confess them to men; and yet in

4. God does promise to raise up this individual, but He does not commit Himself to a specific time. The healing may be instantaneous or it may take weeks, months, or years—or it may not take place until we begin living in eternity with Him.

sin there are two barriers to be removed—the barrier it sets up between us and God, and the barrier it sets up between us and our fellow-men. If both these barriers are to be removed, both kinds of confession must be made.[5]

Second, *praying for one another is essential—practice it!* An appropriate response to your friends' confessions would be to lift them up to the Lord in prayer. Let these companions know that you are willing to enter into their struggle, let them hear your love and support being poured out on their behalf before the throne of God.

Third, *use of medical assistance is imperative—obtain it!* Asking others to pray for your physical healing while ignoring proper medical treatment is not spiritual, it's foolish. Someone may rightly ask, "Why should I pray for your healing if you're not willing to do all that God commands, like seeking medical assistance?"

Fourth, *when healing comes from God—claim it!* Whether or not an illness is the result of personal sin, when God heals, remember to thank Him and give Him the glory!

A Final Word

Did you notice that James never once mentions faith healers? When we're sick, we are commanded to call for the leaders in our local assembly. And it makes no difference what their spiritual gifts are.

We'll close with Chuck Swindoll's conclusion on this important topic.

> I believe in divine healing. I do not believe in divine healers. I believe in faith healing. I do not believe in faith healers. There is a great difference. I believe that God in His sovereign grace and power will in fact reach down in some cases and change a condition. . . . And I am of the conviction that God does that apart from any individual who claims to have certain powers."[6]

5. William Barclay, *The Letters of James and Peter*, rev. ed., The Daily Study Bible series (Philadelphia, Pa.: Westminster Press, 1976), p. 131.

6. Charles R. Swindoll, "Suffering, Sickness, Sin—and Healing," message in *James: Hands-On Christianity* audiocassette series (Plano, Tex.: 2003), JMS07B.

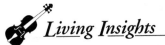 *Living Insights*

Let's take another look at the issues of suffering, sickness, sin, and healing, this time personalizing James's remarks.

Are you suffering? If your circumstances are pressing you hard, then James encourages you to pray and to endure.

If you were to compare yourself to an athlete, would you say you are capable of enduring a marathon of suffering or are you out of breath after only a few strides?

_____

_____

What accounts for the condition you find yourself in?

_____

_____

Read Romans 5:3–5. What does tribulation or suffering bring about?

_____

_____

What does perseverance lead to?

_____

_____

What does proven character produce?

_____

_____

Read James 1:2–4. How should you respond to suffering?

_____

_____

What will suffering produce in your life?

_____

_____

How do these truths increase your suffering stamina?

_____

_____

_____

 ## Questions for Group Discussion

1. The next time you are struggling with prolonged suffering, how will James's words help you to keep running?

2. When you are struggling, how will you lean on the church for support?

3. Who are the people you call when you need prayer? If you don't have many, who could you cultivate a relationship with?

4. If you pray to be healed and your condition continues, how can your sickness help you walk more closely with the Lord?

5. When Jesus was on earth, did He heal everyone who was sick? Why not?

6. Can God's glory be shown through some people being healed on earth and others walking through life without healing? How?

Chapter 15

THE POWER OF
EFFECTIVE KNEELING

James 5:13–18

As far as nicknames go, there aren't many people who would want to be known as "Ol' Camel Knees." But that's exactly what James's friends respectfully called him. And the reason might surprise you, especially since his letter emphasizes the practical aspects of the Christian life. Herbert Lockyer, in his book *All the Men of the Bible*, writes that James

> was a man who believed in the power of prayer. . . .
> Because of his habit of always kneeling in inter-
> cession for the saints, his knees because calloused
> like a camel's; thus he became known as "The Man
> with Camel's Knees."[1]

James was a man of action—a diligent, practical-thinking Christian. But he was also a man of prayer. He marched forth on his knees, taking heaven by storm with fervent, bold, effective prayer.

In our last lesson, we studied the advice of the practical-thinking James on suffering, sickness, sin, and healing. Now, let's go back over some of the same verses and note the exhortation of the camel-kneed James on "the power of effective kneeling."

Instruction of James

The thread of prayer woven into the letter of James begins in chapter 1. Looking back, you may recall the advice James gave those whose faith was being tested and who needed help to endure.

> But if any of you lacks wisdom, let him ask of
> God, who gives to all men generously and without
> reproach, and it will be given to him. (James 1:5)

---

1. Herbert Lockyer, *All the Men of the Bible* (Grand Rapids, Mich.: Zondervan Publishing House, 1958), p. 171.

119

Later, in chapter 4, prayer emerges again, but this time in a context of conflict.

> What is the source of quarrels and conflicts among you? Is not the source your pleasures that wage war in your members? You lust and do not have; so you commit murder. You are envious and cannot obtain; so you fight and quarrel. You do not have because you do not ask. (4:1–2)

It's sad to think how many of us could confess the truth of this last part of verse 2, isn't it? Someone once pictured heaven as having an enormous room with brightly wrapped and beribboned packages in it, each gift having one of our names on it and a little tag that says, "Never delivered to earth, because never requested from earth."

Over and over again in Scripture, we are shown that God wants us to ask because He wants us to have (see Matt. 7:7–11; Heb. 4:16). The topic of our current passage is the matter of asking God certain things because of certain situations.

So let's look at this passage, James 5:13–18, six verses where prayer is mentioned seven times. Within these verses, James brings before us four practical areas where prayer is essential.

When Afflicted . . . Pray!

> Is anyone among you suffering? Then he must pray. (v. 13a)

As we noted in our last lesson, the Greek term for *suffering* here is a broad one that includes not only physical suffering but mental and emotional anguish as well. For those who are in this crucible of pain, James's counsel is to respond not with complaints (v. 9) or swearing (v. 12), but with continual prayer.[2]

What can we expect in return for our prayers? It's important to note that James does not promise specific relief, although relief may come. Nor does he guarantee that we will understand the reason behind our suffering. So why pray? Are our hot tears and pained cries all in vain? C. H. Spurgeon addressed this question.

> We ought not to tolerate for a minute the ghastly and grievous thought that God will not answer prayer. His nature, as manifested in Christ Jesus,

2. The command to pray is in the present tense, which signifies to pray continuously.

demands it. He has revealed Himself in the gospel, as a God of love, full of grace and truth; and how can He refuse to help those of His creatures who humbly in His own appointed way seek His face and favour? . . .

Still remember that prayer is always to be offered in submission to God's will; that when we say, God heareth prayer, we do not intend by that, that He always gives us literally what we ask for. We do mean, however, this, that He gives us what is best for us; and that if He does not give us the mercy we ask for in silver, He bestows it upon us in gold. If He doth not take away the thorn in the flesh, yet He saith, "My grace is sufficient for thee," and that comes to the same in the end.[3]

So the role of prayer in our suffering is to place our aching burden into the tender hands of God, who will in turn renew our inner strength and make the load easier to bear.

When Sick . . . Pray!

The second situation in which James calls for prayer involves those who are bedridden and without strength due to a serious physical illness.

Is anyone among you sick? Then he must call for the elders of the church and they are to pray over him, anointing him with oil in the name of the Lord. (v. 14)

If we're sick, we should follow three steps, according to this verse. First, we should make the spiritual leaders of the church aware of our need.

Second, and this step is rooted in the word *anoint*, we should see a doctor and ask for prayer. In our last lesson we saw that the Greek term for *anointing* here refers to rubbing in oil for medicinal purposes. So in James's day this meant that the leaders were to come and administer two things: proper medicine and prayer. For us today, James is simply saying that the elders should make sure we're getting proper medical treatment and pray for us.

3. C. H. Spurgeon, "The Golden Key of Prayer," in *Twelve Sermons on Prayer* (Grand Rapids, Mich.: Baker Book House, 1990), pp. 10, 13.

Third, because the medical treatment and prayer for healing should be done "in the name of the Lord," we need to leave the results of the medicine and prayers in God's hands.

When Corrupted by Sin . . . Pray!

> Therefore, confess your sins to one another; and pray for one another, so that you may be healed. (v. 16a)

Remember, James has just dealt with those who were bedridden. According to the context of verses 13–16, these people were ill as a result of unconfessed sin in their lives. Beginning in verse 16, however, James turns a corner, as evidenced by his use of "therefore" and his switch from "him" to "you." *Therefore* lets us know that James is about to make an important point, and *you* takes this point out of the theoretical and into the personal. In short, James is advising that, to keep sin from making us ill, we need to *confess* our sins to one another regularly and *pray* continuously.

Before we move to the next point in our study, let's pause for a moment to remove some theological barnacles that have accumulated on the timeless truth of verse 16.

Briefly, there are some who say this verse is talking about salvation. However, James is addressing believers, and the subject is healing. Others teach that verse 16 is talking about confession to a priest. But the words "one another" show that James simply means believers. Finally, James is recommending that we not bare our sins indiscriminately before an entire group. There is a tone of privacy in his "one another" counsel. There are certain matters we should not suffer alone. They should be shared and prayed about with a close brother or sister.

When Specific Needs Occur . . . Pray!

James reveals the last area in which prayer is essential in the second half of verse 16:

> The effective prayer of a righteous man can accomplish much.

The Greek term for *prayer* used here is *deesis*, meaning "specific prayer based on specific needs." It's the only time in his letter that James uses this word.

In addition, he intensifies his statement by using two qualifying adjectives, *effective* and *much*. The Greek root for effective is *energeo*, from which we get the word *energy*. It has to do with adding an ingredient that turns something average into something fantastic.

For instance, if a speech is lacking *energeo*, it's just another speech. But if a speech has this quality, it's dynamite!

So what does it mean to pray "effectively"? It involves knowing and praying in accordance with Scripture. It also includes being specific. Learn to deal directly with the issues you pray about by asking for specific results. This does not mean, however, that we require God to meet our deadlines. Faith involves waiting on God's timing without doubting. And finally, *energeo* prayer embraces an absolute and unshakable faith that God hears and answers prayer.

The result of effective prayer is that it will "accomplish much," just as it did in Elijah's life.

> Elijah was a man with a nature like ours, and he prayed earnestly that it might not rain; and it did not rain on the earth for three years and six months. Then he prayed again, and the sky poured rain, and the earth produced its fruits. (vv. 17–18)

Elijah was cut out of the same cloth as the rest of us. The only difference between Elijah and many of us is that he practiced effective praying. He prayed in accordance with God's will, he was specific, and he prayed in faith (see 1 Kings 17–18).

The Relevance of James

Looking back on these major areas of prayer that James mentions, we can find four specific applications for us today.

First, *prayer is to be continuous.* Prayer is not something we should practice only at mealtimes or in moments of panic or when we've exhausted all our own efforts to meet our needs. James repeatedly uses the present tense throughout these verses, exhorting us to pray continuously or, as the apostle Paul said, "without ceasing" (1 Thess. 5:17). The adverb for *without ceasing* in Greek is like a hacking cough—something that you are constantly reminded of throughout the day. The Puritans described this kind of constant prayerful attitude as practicing the presence of God—keeping alert to His presence throughout the day.

Second, *prayer is designed for every part of life.* Affliction, sickness, sin, specific needs—nothing is too big or too small for prayer. If it's a concern—ask!

Third, *prayer is not a substitute for responsible and intelligent action*. Remember that the one who is sick is supposed to contact the elders and seek proper medical treatment. If you're not willing to see a doctor and take the right kind of medicine, don't ask people to pray for you. And remember that healing some physical illnesses may involve confessing sins and seeking forgiveness.

Fourth, *prayer is not for the perfect, but for the imperfect*. Because we are imperfect and have needs, we need to pray. Elijah wasn't perfect, but he was persistent about prayer. So was James—"Ol' Camel Knees." What nickname would you use to describe yourself in light of your prayer life?

Before we close and the daily demands of life distract you from what you've just learned, pause and meditate on the these powerful words from Clarence Edward Macartney:

> What is the word that unites far separated souls around one common mercy seat? What is the word that brings man's storm-driven ship into the haven of safety and peace? What is the word that turns back the shadow of death on the face of life's dial? What is the word that gives songs in the night and that lifts the load of guilt from the conscience-smitten heart? What is the word that puts a sword in our hand when we face temptation? What is the word that gives us strength to bear our daily burdens?
>
> . . . What is the word that makes us co-workers with God in the coming of His kingdom? . . .
>
> . . . What is the word that companions the soul in its hours of loneliness and that comforts it in the day of sorrow? What is the word that sets a map of forgiveness and reconciliation in the window for the prodigal and the wandered? What is the word that brings the eternal world to view? . . . What is the word that makes the angels rejoice when they hear it on the lips of a contrite sinner? . . .
>
> That mighty, all prevailing, God-conquering word is prayer. "The effectual fervent prayer of a righteous man availeth much" (James 5:16).[4]

---

4. Clarence Edward Macartney, "The Word That Conquers God," in *Classic Sermons on Prayer*, comp. Warren W. Wiersbe (Grand Rapids, Mich.: Kregal Publications, 1987), pp. 9–10.

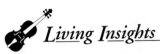

Living Insights

James 4:2 says that we do not have because we do not ask. Have you ever been troubled by something and talked to everyone but God about it? Why does it sometimes seem easier to ask people to solve our problems before we ask God to solve them?

_____

_____

_____

What issues in your life are concerning you right now?

_____

_____

_____

Take a few moments to ask God to help you with these issues. Write your requests to Him on the lines below.

_____

_____

_____

_____

_____

Look back at your requests in the weeks to come and continue to pray about these issues as long as they are causing you concern. As you pray, write your answered prayers on the following lines.

_____

_____

_____

_____

_____

_____

_____

_____

_____

_____

_____

If your prayers seem to fall on deaf ears, be patient. God may be waiting to answer your prayers to reveal Himself to you in His time.

 ## Questions _for_ Group Discussion

1. Does James 4:2 imply that we can have anything we ask for?

2. How do we know if we are asking for things in God's will?

3. Why is prayer often our last resort rather than our first defense?

4. How can you grow in your prayer life?

5. How can you keep from getting distracted while you pray?

6. How will praying align your heart with God's heart?

7. What prayers has God answered in your life this week?

Chapter 16

HOW TO HANDLE
STRAYING SAINTS

James 5:19–20

Have you ever rescued someone from drowning? If so, you know how victims often fight their rescuers in the hysteria of that terrifying moment. The same is often true when an attempt is made to rescue those who are floundering spiritually because their faith has suffered shipwreck.

Author and teacher Howard Hendricks tells the story of a young man who strayed from the Lord but was finally brought back by the help of a friend who really loved him. When there was full repentance and restoration, Dr. Hendricks asked this Christian how it felt while he was out at sea, in deep water, deep trouble, and all his friends were on the shoreline hurling biblical accusations at him about justice, penalty, and wrong-doing. He answered:

> "There was one man who swam out to get me and he would not let me go. I fought him . . . [but] he pushed aside my fighting and he grasped me and he put a life jacket around me and he took me to shore. And he, by the grace of God, was the reason I was restored. He would not let me go."[1]

James doesn't want us to let anyone go either. Throughout his epistle, he has stressed the need for a faith that works. Now he reminds us not to let go of those who have grown weary and strayed.

Comparing James with Jesus

As a backdrop to this study, let's compare James's and Jesus' teachings on the subject of judging. To start, turn back to James 4:11–12.

> Do not speak against one another, brethren. He who speaks against a brother or judges his brother,

---

1. As retold by Charles R. Swindoll, in a sermon titled "Set Me Free," given at the First Evangelical Free Church of Fullerton, California, January 25, 1981.

speaks against the law, and judges the law; but if you judge the law, you are not a doer of the law, but a judge of it. There is only one Lawgiver and Judge, the One who is able to save and to destroy; but who are you who judge your neighbor?

In this passage, James is not prohibiting Christians from confronting those who have strayed; rather, he is warning against believers who maliciously slander others. Jesus underscored this same point in Matthew 7:

> "Do not judge so that you will not be judged. For in the way you judge, you will be judged; and by your standard of measure, it will be measured to you. Why do you look at the speck that is in your brother's eye, but do not notice the log that is in your own eye? Or how can you say to your brother, 'Let me take the speck out of your eye,' and behold, the log is in your own eye?" (vv. 1–4)

The conclusion many Christians have drawn from these passages can be boiled down to just three words: Do not judge!

But what about those times when a Christian brother or sister strays from the Lord? Shouldn't we attempt to rescue those whose faith has suffered shipwreck? Or do we simply let them perish? The climax of Jesus' words in our Matthew passage answers this seeming dilemma.

> "You hypocrite, first take the log out of your own eye, and then you will see clearly to take the speck out of your brother's eye." (v. 5)

According to Jesus, there is a place for taking specks out of other Christians' eyes. But remember, there are few places in our bodies more sensitive to touch than the eye. And just as removing something from the physical eye requires extreme sensitivity, so does attempting to remove the spiritual speck from our brother's or sister's eye. So Jesus is not condoning those who feel "called" to criticism. Rather, He is welcoming the help of those who are willing to have their own spiritual eyes cleared before rescuing others.

Understanding James's Counsel

To learn more about the techniques involved in spiritual eye surgery, let's turn now to James's closing words.

> My brethren, if any among you strays from the truth and one turns him back, let him know that he who turns a sinner from the error of his way will save his soul from death, and will cover a multitude of sins. (James 5:19–20)

Four important questions arise from these verses.

Important Questions

First, *about whom is the counsel addressed?* At a glance, it appears as though James is speaking about saving lost souls from hell. However, the words "my brethren" and "among you" indicate that he is addressing believers.

Second, *what has occurred that would cause James to write these words?* Most likely, someone has strayed from the truth. The word *strays* in Greek is *planao,* from which we get the word *planet.* The heavenly bodies seemed to the ancient Greeks to wander in the sky. Likewise, when Christians stray from the truth, they wander from the prescribed course they once knew.[2]

Third, *from what has the person strayed?* The truth. Commentator Spiro Zodhiates expands on what straying from the truth involves.

> The truth of which James speaks is naturally the person and work of Jesus Christ. He does not refer to an abstract philosophical or theological system, but to Christ Himself, who said, "I am the way, the truth, and the life" (John 14:6). . . . Of course, the word "truth" here also means all that Christ taught and instituted. It is His whole doctrinal and practical teaching—not the teaching of any particular church or denomination, but of Christ. And where is this teaching to be found? In the Word of God, in the Bible.[3]

---

2. Again, the implication here is that James is talking to believers, because only those who have intimately known the truth can stray from it. Unbelievers cannot stray from something they have never known.

3. Spiros Zodhiates, *The Behavior of Belief* (Grand Rapids, Mich.: William B. Eerdmans Publishing Co., 1959), p. 217.

Fourth, *what should be done?* Now we come to the most sensitive part: removing the speck from our brother's eye. When Christians willfully stray from the truth, James says that one must turn them back, meaning *any* Christian with a clear eye—not just church leaders—must help turn around those who stray. Don't ignore them or hurl criticisms from a distance, as some did to that young Christian Dr. Hendricks has talked about. Swim out after them and don't let them go!

Proper Attitude

Now that we've considered the action we must take, let's turn to Galatians 6 for a close look at the proper attitude we need.

> Brethren, even if anyone is caught in any trespass, you who are spiritual, restore such a one in a spirit of gentleness; each one looking to yourself, so that you too will not be tempted. Bear one another's burdens, and thereby fulfill the law of Christ. For if anyone thinks he is something when he is nothing, he deceives himself. (Gal. 6:1–3)

To qualify for helping restore others to the truth, we must first be filled with the Spirit and not controlled by the flesh. We must seek the Spirit's help in removing the logs in our own eyes before we attempt to remove them from others. Only those who are spiritual—who approach such an operation in complete dependence upon the Spirit—need apply for the job.

The second qualification Paul mentions is gentleness. Carnal Christians are usually extremely sensitive to criticism. To approach them with a harsh, critical spirit only ensures failure and rejection. But a gentle spirit encourages those who are floundering to relax and be reconciled to God.

Third, before we rush off into deep water to rescue someone, we should check to be sure we are equipped with an attitude of humility—"looking to yourself, so that you too will not be tempted." Misjudging the depth of the problem or overestimating our ability to handle it could quickly leave us floundering as well.

Removing specks is not a pleasurable task. There's no delight in rescuing someone who is thrashing and kicking against your every effort to help. In fact, those who are truly humble are often reluctant to step in, knowing that they don't have the power in themselves to pull the other person to safety. Nevertheless, the humble do wade out, slowly . . . prayerfully, because of a genuine love from the Father.

Operation Restoration

Thus far we've covered the action and attitude involved in handling saints who stray. Now let's go back to James 5 and see what happens when they are restored.

> Let him know that he who turns a sinner from the error of his way will save his soul from death, and will cover a multitude of sins. (James 5:20)

The first result is that the straying saint's soul will be saved "from death." The word *death* could mean that if this individual had not turned back to the Lord, he or she may have died under divine discipline. It is more likely, however, that James means death in a broad, metaphorical sense. When we turn straying saints back to the Lord, we rescue their souls from a deathlike existence of loneliness, bitterness, anguish, and guilt.

The second result is that we "cover a multitude of sins." When someone is brought back into the fold through confession and repentance, Christ's forgiveness covers this formerly lost sheep completely.

Summary and Application

Throughout his letter James has pinpointed specific areas in which Christians have begun to slip: doubting during trials, blaming when tempted, anger and prejudice, sterile intellectualism, a loose tongue, jealousy, arrogance, being judgmental, planning without God, taking advantage of others because of wealth, and lack of prayer—to name a few. For these five chapters, James has been coming to our rescue. Now let's close by crystallizing his counsel about our rescuing one another.

First, there are definite occasions when we are to be involved in removing specks from others' eyes. Second, the entire process must be under the direction of the Holy Spirit. Third, the motive or attitude is as important as the action. And fourth, when we are prompted by the Lord, we should not feel reluctant or out of place about confronting others. Remember that you are saving that person from death and covering a multitude of sins. Don't let go!

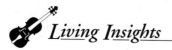

Living Insights

In Matthew 7:1–2, Jesus clearly commands us not to condemn another person. And yet He doesn't command us to condone another person's sin. According to verse 5 of Matthew 7, what do you need to do before addressing another person's fault?

_____

_____

_____

In Galatians 6:1 Paul exhorts,

> Brethren, even if anyone is caught up in any trespass, you who are spiritual restore such a one in a spirit of gentleness; each one looking to yourself, so that you too will not be tempted.

Before confronting a brother or sister, examine your own heart. According to Galatians 5:22–23, James 3:17, and 1 Corinthians 13, what does it mean to have a spiritual attitude?

_____

_____

_____

Look at Matthew 5:5, 11:29, 21:5, and John 8:1–11. What does Jesus say and model about gentleness?

_____

_____

_____

Read Matthew 20:25b–28. What motive should you have when confronting another?

_____

_____

_____

Is your spirit attuned to God in a tender and humble manner? If not, should you confront your brother or sister?

_____

_____

_____

 ## Questions for Group Discussion

1. Should you ever confront someone out of anger or vindication? What motives should you have?

2. If you are not spiritually motivated to confront another person with gentleness and in humility, what should you do?

3. How will prayer help you prepare your heart for confrontation with another?

4. If you anticipate that the person you're confronting might respond to you harshly, should you still confront?

5. Some people received Jesus when He confronted them, and others rejected Him. Did their rejection keep Him from speaking? Why not?

6. Is it okay to confront someone you know but are not close to?

7. Is it true that godly confrontation is a loving act? If so, why are most Christians afraid to do it? If you allow a brother or sister to remain in sin and say nothing, are you showing him or her love?

BOOKS FOR
PROBING FURTHER

Commentaries on James

Barclay, William. *The Letters of James and Peter*. Revised edition. The Daily Bible Study series. Philadelphia, Pa.: Westminster Press, 1976.

Hughes, R. Kent. *James, Preaching the Word*. Wheaton, Ill.: Good News Publishing, 1991.

Moo, Douglas. *James*. Tyndale New Testament Commentary. Grand Rapids, Mich.: Eerdman's Publishing Company, 1985.

Moo, Douglas. *The Letter of James*. Pillar New Testament Commentary. Grand Rapids, Mich.: Eerdman's Publishing Company, 2000.

Motyer, J. A. *The Message of James*. The Bible Speaks Today series. Downers Grove, Ill.: InterVarsity Press, 1985.

Books That Focus on Key Themes in James

Colson, Charles. *Kingdoms in Conflict*. Grand Rapids, Mich.: William Morrow and Zondervan Publishing House, 1987.

Colson, Charles. *Loving God*. Grand Rapids, Mich.: Zondervan Publishing House, 1983.

Geisler, Norman L. *Christian Ethics*. Grand Rapids, Mich.: Baker Book House, 1989.

Hunter, W. Bingham. *The God Who Hears*. Downers Grove, Ill.: InterVarsity Press, 1986.

Maines, Karen Burton. *You Are What You Say*. Grand Rapids, Mich.: Zondervan Publishing House, 1988.

Neff, David, ed. *The Midas Trap*. The Christianity Today Series. Wheaton, Ill.: Victor Books, 1990.

Stott, John. *Involvement. Volume 1, Being a Responsible Christian in a Non-Christian Society.* Old Tappan, N.J.: Fleming H. Revell Co., 1985.

Stott, John. *Involvement. Volume 2, Social and Sexual Relationships in the Modern World.* A Crucial Questions Book. Old Tappan, N.J.: Fleming H. Revell Co., 1985.

Wright, H. Norman. *Communication: Key to Your Marriage.* Glendale, Calif.: G/L Publications, Regal Books, 1974.

Yancey, Philip. *Where Is God When It Hurts?* Grand Rapids, Mich.: Zondervan Publishing House, 1977.

Some of the books listed may be out of print or available only through a library. For those currently available, please contact your local Christian bookstore. Books by Charles R. Swindoll can be obtained through the Insight for Living Resource Center, as can many books by other authors. Just call the Insight for Living office that serves you.

Insight for Living also has Bible study guides available on many books of the Bible as well as on a variety of topics, Bible characters, and contemporary issues. For more information, see the ordering instructions that follow and contact the office that serves you.

Ordering Information

James: Hands-on Christianity

If you would like to order additional Bible study guides, purchase the audiocassette series that accompanies this guide, or request our product catalogs, please contact the office that serves you.

United States and International Locations:

Insight for Living
Post Office Box 269000
Plano, TX 75026-9000

1-800-772-8888, 24 hours a day, seven days a week (U.S. contacts) International constituents may contact the U.S. office through mail queries.

Canada:

Insight for Living Ministries
Post Office Box 2510
Vancouver, BC, Canada V6B 3W7

1-800-663-7639, 24 hours a day, seven days a week
InfoCanada@insight.org

Australia:

Insight for Living, Inc.
Suite 4, 43 Railway Rd.
Blackburn, VIC 3130, Australia

Toll-free 1800 772 888 or (03) 9877-4277, 8:30 A.M. to 5:00 P.M., Monday through Friday
iflaus@insight.org

World Wide Web:
www.insight.org

Bible Study Guide Subscription Program

Bible study guide subscriptions are available. Please call or write the office nearest you to find out how you can receive our Bible study guides on a regular basis.